W9-CCZ-000

COOKING WITH

FOIL

Publications International, Ltd.
Favorite Brand Name Recipes at www.fbnr.com

Pictured on the front cover: Chicken with Cornbread Dumplings *(page 76).*
Pictured on the back cover *(clockwise from top left):* Grilled Potato Salad
(page 154), BBQ Shortribs with Cola Sauce *(page 12)* and Mango-Banana
Foster *(page 182).*

ISBN: 0-7853-9852-X

Library of Congress Control Number: 2003098912

Manufactured in China.

8 7 6 5 4 3 2 1

Microwave Cooking: Microwave ovens vary in wattage. Use the cooking times
as guidelines and check for doneness before adding more time.

Preparation/Cooking Times: Preparation times are based on the approximate
amount of time required to assemble the recipe before cooking, baking, chilling
or serving. These times include preparation steps such as measuring, chopping
and mixing. The fact that some preparations and cooking can be done
simultaneously is taken into account. Preparation of optional ingredients and
serving suggestions is not included.

Contents

page 128

page 14

page 183

Simply Delicious Foil Recipes

It's one of those days—everyone's on a different dinner schedule and you're wondering how you can avoid serving reheated, dried-out meals to the latecomers. Let foil packets come to the rescue! With packet cooking you can prepare individual servings, wrap them in foil and hold them in the refrigerator until you're ready to cook—no more reheating food for dinner stragglers. You can create delicious dinners easily and quickly and keep cleanup to a minimum when you cook in foil.

Cooking with Foil includes over of recipes for cooking or grilling in foil packets. In addition, discover the convenience of cooking in foil bags, lining baking pans with foil, covering dishes with nonstick foil and baking in foil cups. You'll be surprised how quick and easy foil cooking can be.

Oven Roasted Potatoes and Onions with Herbs, page 160

Foil Packet Cooking

What is foil packet cooking? Wrap ingredients in foil to create packets, then cook them in a hot oven or on the grill. Packets can serve one or more. Recipes for one or two can be prepared in most toaster ovens, which will help to keep the kitchen cool and save energy. Vegetable packets can be tossed on the grill while the steaks or burgers are grilling. You'll love the convenience of this cooking method. Packets can be prepared ahead of time and cooked when needed. There are no pots and pans to scrub and the oven stays clean, too. You can even customize individual packets for fussy eaters—for example, simply prepare one packet without the mushrooms that one family member dislikes.

Spicy Lasagna Rolls, page 60

Packet Basics

◆ Measure and tear off a foil sheet(s) as directed in the recipe and place it on the countertop.

◆ Spray the foil with nonstick cooking spray or grease with butter or margarine as directed in the recipe. In most cases a light spraying is sufficient, but sticky or sugary foods may require a generous coating.

◆ Preheat the oven, toaster oven or grill.

◆ Place the ingredients in the center of the foil sheets as the recipe directs.

Double fold foil and crimp tightly to seal.

◆ Wrap foil around the ingredients, leaving room for heat to circulate. Bring the two sides together above the food; double fold the foil and crimp to seal as shown in the above photograph.

Double fold each end of packet and crimp tightly to seal.

◆ Double fold the remaining ends and crimp to seal the packet (above photograph).

◆ Place the foil packets on a baking sheet, toaster oven tray or a baking pan with 1-inch-high sides.

◆ Bake the packets on the baking sheet on the center rack as directed. Or, slide the packets onto the grill.

◆ Remove packets from the oven. The foil packets will be very hot so use oven mitts when handling them. Carefully open one end of each packet to avoid the escaping steam. Allow some of the steam to escape before completely opening the packet. Check the food for doneness; rewrap and return to the oven if the food isn't completely cooked.

◆ Transfer the contents of the packets to serving plates or a serving dish. When cooking single-serve packets of food, you may eat right out of the packet if you wish.

Large Foil Bags

Foil bags large enough to hold a turkey are available at most supermarkets. Use these bags for large items such as turkeys, roasting chickens, beef roasts and pork roasts. Add vegetables to the bag and you have almost an entire meal prepared quickly and conveniently. Cleanup is easy, too.

Other Uses of Foil in the Kitchen

Lining baking pans with foil: When roasting meat or vegetables, first line the baking pan with foil to minimize cleanup. When baking bar cookies or brownies, line the baking pan with foil, allowing the edges of the foil sheet to overhang the edges of the pan. Grease the foil. After the bars or brownies are cool, simply lift them out of the pan using the foil.

Lining cookie sheets with foil: Place a sheet of foil on the cookie sheet when making cookies. Grease the foil if the recipe recommends greasing the cookie sheet. Place cookie dough on the foil and bake as directed. After removing cookies from the oven, slide the foil off the cookie sheet onto a wire rack or the countertop. Cool the cookie sheet and reuse it with another sheet of foil—the cookie sheet remains clean.

Covering with foil: Nonstick foil can be used to cover baking pans and casseroles during baking. The melted cheese from a lasgana won't stick to the foil and your meal remains intact.

Cooking in a slow cooker: To easily lift a meatloaf or a casserole dish out of a slow cooker, make foil handles according to the following directions:

Crisscross the strips of foil like spokes of a wheel.

Cut three 18×3-inch strips of heavy-duty foil. Crisscross the strips so they resemble the spokes of a wheel. Place the dish or food in the center of the strips.

Pull the foil strips up and over the food. Use the strips to lower the food into the slow cooker. Leave the strips in while you cook so you can easily lift the food out again when its finished cooking.

Pull foil strips up and over the food.

Foil Bake Cups

Foil bake cups, like paper bake cups, are available in several sizes to line muffin pans when making muffins or cupcakes. The added bonus of foil bake cups is that they are usually rigid enough to be used without muffin pans. Simply place the bake cups in a shallow baking pan.

Individual Chocolate Coconut Cheesecakes, page 186

Disposable Foil Baking Pans

Disposable foil baking pans are readily available in many sizes. Use them in place of a roasting pan for a holiday turkey or a Sunday-supper roast. Use them for transporting your favorite dish to the next pot-luck dinner or picnic. There's no need to worry about searching for your casserole dish when the meal's over. Bake bar cookies, brownies and sheet cakes in disposable foil pans if you plan to ship them to friends or family or take them to a bake sale.

Cooking with Foil

From tasty main dishes, like Salmon with Warm Mango Salsa and Apricot Pork Chops and Dressing, to taste-tempting side dishes and quick-to-fix meal finales, like Cinnamon-Raisin-Banana Bread Pudding and Easy Gingerbread, you'll discover a variety of recipes that will simplify dinner preparation whether you're cooking for one or an on-the-go family. So roll out the foil and enjoy an easy-to-make, home-cooked meal tonight!

BBQ Shortribs with Cola Sauce, page 12

quick fix

Main Dishes

BBQ Shortribs with Cola Sauce

   1 large (17×15 inches) foil bag
   1 can (12 ounces) regular cola
   1 can (6 ounces) tomato paste
   ¾ cup honey
   ½ cup cider vinegar
   1 teaspoon salt
   2 cloves garlic, minced
     Dash hot pepper sauce (optional)
   4 pounds beef shortribs, cut into 2-inch lengths

1. Preheat oven to 450°F. Place foil bag in 1-inch deep jelly-roll pan. Spray inside of bag with nonstick cooking spray. Dust with flour.

2. To prepare sauce, combine cola, tomato paste, honey, vinegar, salt, garlic and hot pepper sauce, if desired, in 2-quart saucepan. Bring to a boil over medium-high heat. Reduce heat slightly and cook, stirring occasionally, until slightly reduced, about 15 minutes.

3. Dip each shortrib in sauce. Place ribs in single layer in prepared foil bag. Ladle additional 1 cup sauce into bag. Seal bag by folding open end twice.

4. Bake 1 hour 15 minutes or until ribs are cooked through. Carefully cut open bag. *Makes 4 to 6 servings*

BBQ Shortribs with Cola Sauce

Salmon with Warm Mango Salsa

1¼ pounds salmon fillet, about 1 inch thick
½ teaspoon paprika
⅛ teaspoon ground red pepper
4 sheets (18×12 inches) heavy-duty foil, lightly sprayed with nonstick cooking spray
2 medium mangoes, peeled, seeded and cut into ¾-inch pieces
½ medium red bell pepper, chopped
1 jalapeño pepper,* seeded and finely chopped
2 tablespoons chopped fresh parsley
1 tablespoon frozen orange-pineapple juice concentrate or orange juice concentrate, thawed

*Jalapeño peppers can sting and irritate the skin; wear rubber gloves when handling peppers and do not touch eyes. Wash hands after handling peppers.

1. Prepare grill for direct cooking.

2. Rinse salmon under cold running water; pat dry with paper towels. Cut salmon into 4 serving-size pieces. Place one piece salmon, skin side down, on each sheet of foil. Combine paprika and red pepper in small bowl. Rub on tops of salmon pieces.

3. Toss together mangoes, bell pepper, jalapeño pepper, parsley and juice concentrate. Spoon onto salmon pieces.

4. Double-fold sides and ends of foil to seal packets, leaving head space for heat circulation. Place on baking sheet.

5. Slide packets off baking sheet onto grill grid. Grill, covered, over medium-high coals 9 to 11 minutes or until fish flakes when tested with fork. Carefully open one end of each packet to allow steam to escape. Open packets and transfer to serving plates.   *Makes 4 servings*

Salmon with Warm Mango Salsa

Stuffed Apricot Pork Chops

¾ **cup seasoned stuffing mix**
¾ **cup chopped dried apricots**
2 **tablespoons chopped red onion**
2 **tablespoons slivered almonds**
2 **tablespoons chicken broth**
4 **(1-inch thick) center-cut pork chops**
   Salt and pepper
1 **teaspoon paprika**
4 **sheets (18×12 inches) heavy-duty foil, lightly sprayed with**
   nonstick cooking spray
¼ **cups apricot preserves**
1 **teaspoon Dijon-style mustard**
1 **teaspoon soy sauce**

1. Combine stuffing mix, apricots, onion, almonds and broth in medium bowl.

2. Place pork chops on cutting board, cut horizontal pocket in each chop. Season cut surfaces with salt and pepper. Place stuffing mixture in pork chops. Rub both sides of pork chop with paprika. Place each pork chop on foil sheet.

3. Combine apricot preserves, mustard and soy sauce in small bowl. Spoon about 1 tablespoon preserve mixture on top of each chop. Double fold sides and ends of foil to seal packet, leaving head space for heat circulation. Place packets on baking sheet.

4. Bake 20 to 23 minutes or until pork is cooked through.

Makes 4 servings

Cherry-Glazed Chicken

1 (2½- to 3-pound) broiler-fryer chicken, cut up (or 6 chicken
    breast halves, skinned and boned)
½ cup milk
½ cup all-purpose flour
1 teaspoon dried thyme
    Salt and pepper, to taste
1 to 2 tablespoons vegetable oil
1 (16-ounce) can unsweetened tart cherries
¼ cup brown sugar
¼ cup granulated sugar
1 teaspoon prepared yellow mustard

Rinse chicken; pat dry with paper towels. Pour milk into a shallow container. In another container, combine flour, thyme, salt and pepper. Dip chicken first in milk, then in flour mixture; coat evenly. Heat oil in a large skillet. Add chicken; brown on all sides. Place chicken in 13×9×2-inch baking dish. Bake, covered with aluminum foil, in preheated 350°F oven 30 minutes.

Meanwhile, drain cherries, reserving ½ cup juice. Combine cherry juice, brown sugar and granulated sugar in small saucepan; mix well. Bring mixture to a boil over medium heat. Add mustard; mix well. Cook 5 minutes, or until sauce is syrupy. Stir in cherries.

After chicken has cooked 30 minutes, remove baking dish from oven and carefully remove foil cover. Spoon hot cherry mixture evenly over chicken. Bake, uncovered, 15 minutes, or until chicken is done. Serve immediately. *Makes 6 servings*

Favorite recipe from *Cherry Marketing Institute*

Spinach-Stuffed Turkey Meat Loaf

1 sheet (24×12 inches) heavy-duty foil, lightly sprayed with
    nonstick cooking spray
1 pound ground turkey
1 cup finely chopped onion
½ cup unseasoned dry breadcrumbs
½ cup finely chopped red bell pepper
2 eggs
2 tablespoons bacon bits
1 teaspoon dried thyme leaves
½ teaspoon salt
½ teaspoon black pepper
1 package (10 ounces) frozen chopped spinach, thawed and
    squeezed dry
⅓ cup sour cream
⅓ cup shredded Swiss cheese

1. Preheat oven to 450°F. Center foil over 9×5×3-inch loaf pan. Gently ease foil into pan; leaving a 1-inch overhang on sides of pan and 5-inch overhang on each end. Generously spray foil with nonstick cooking spray.

2. Combine turkey, onion, breadcrumbs, bell pepper, eggs, bacon bits, thyme, salt and black pepper in medium bowl; mix well.

3. Place about 3 cups turkey mixture into prepared pan, packing down lightly and making an indentation, end to end, with back of large spoon.

4. Combine spinach, sour cream and cheese in medium bowl. Spoon into indentation. Cover with remaining turkey mixture, packing down lightly. Fold foil over sides to cover completely; crimp foil, leaving head space for heat circulation.

5. Bake about 50 minutes or until cooked through. Let stand, covered, 10 minutes. Unwrap and slice into 1-inch slices.   *Makes 8 servings*

Chicken Parmesan

2 boneless skinless chicken breasts
2 sheets (18×12 inches) heavy-duty foil, lightly sprayed with
    nonstick cooking spray
 Salt and black pepper
1 cup pasta sauce
½ cup chopped onion
8 slices zucchini, quartered
¼ cup (1 ounce) shredded mozzarella cheese
2 tablespoons grated Parmesan cheese
    Hot cooked spaghetti or linguine (optional)

1. Preheat toaster oven or oven to 450°F.

2. Place one chicken breast in center of each sheet of foil. Season to taste with salt and pepper.

3. Combine pasta sauce, onion and zucchini. Pour half of sauce mixture over each chicken breast. Sprinkle with cheeses. Double fold sides and ends of foil to seal packets, leaving head space for heat circulation. Place packets on toaster oven tray or baking sheet.

4. Bake 16 to 18 minutes until chicken is no longer pink in center. Remove from oven. Carefully open one end of each foil packet to allow steam to escape. Open packets and transfer contents to serving plates. Serve with spaghetti, if desired. *Makes 2 servings*

Chef's Suggestion

To save time, purchase already sliced zucchini and chopped onion from the supermarket salad bar.

Chicken Parmesan

Ham Meat Loaf with Horseradish Sauce

1½ pounds meat loaf mix* or ground beef
½ pound cooked ham, finely chopped
1 cup plain dry bread crumbs
1 cup finely chopped onion
2 large eggs, slightly beaten
½ cup chili sauce or ketchup
1 teaspoon plus ⅛ teaspoon salt, divided
½ teaspoon caraway seeds
¼ teaspoon black pepper
½ cup sour cream
3 tablespoons thinly sliced green onions
1 tablespoon prepared horseradish
1 tablespoon spicy brown or coarse-grained mustard

*Meat loaf mix is a combination of ground beef, pork and veal; see your meat retailer or make your own with 1 pound lean ground beef, ¼ pound ground pork and ¼ pound ground veal.

Slow Cooker Directions

1. Combine meat loaf mix, ham, bread crumbs, onion, eggs, chili sauce, 1 teaspoon salt, caraway seeds and pepper in large bowl; mix well. Shape meat mixture into 7-inch round loaf.

2. Prepare foil handles for slow cooker (see below). Place meat loaf on top of foil strips. Using strips, place meat loaf into slow cooker. Cover; cook on LOW 4 to 4½ hours or until meat thermometer inserted into center of meat loaf reads 165°F. Use foil strips to remove meat loaf from slow cooker. Let stand 5 minutes.

3. Meanwhile, combine sour cream, green onions, horseradish, mustard and remaining ⅛ teaspoon salt in small bowl; mix well. Cut meat loaf into wedges; serve with horseradish sauce.   *Makes 8 servings*

Foil Handles: Tear off three 18×3-inch strips of heavy foil or use regular foil folded to double thickness. Crisscross foil strips in spoke design.

Prep Time: 20 minutes
Cook Time: 4 to 4½ hours

Dilled Salmon in Foil

2 skinless salmon fillets (4 to 6 ounces each)
2 tablespoons butter or margarine, melted
1 tablespoon lemon juice
1 tablespoon chopped fresh dill
1 tablespoon chopped shallots

1. Preheat oven to 400°F. Cut 2 pieces aluminum foil into 12-inch squares; fold squares in half diagonally and cut into half heart shapes. Open foil; place fish fillet on one side of each heart.

2. Combine butter and lemon juice in small cup; drizzle over fish. Sprinkle with dill, shallots and salt and pepper to taste.

3. Fold foil hearts in half. Beginning at top of heart, fold edges together, 2 inches at a time. At tip of heart, fold foil over to seal.

4. Bake fish about 10 minutes or until fish flakes easily when tested with fork. To serve, cut an "X" through top layer of foil and fold back points to display contents.   *Makes 2 servings*

Prep and Cook Time: 20 minutes

Chef's Suggestion

Although salmon has a higher fat content than most fish, it is still very nutritious. Salmon's fat content is made up primarily of omega-3 fatty acids. There is a wealth of research available today that links consumption of omega-3 fatty acids with the reduced risk of heart attack and heart disease.

Memphis Pork Ribs

   1 tablespoon chili powder
   1 tablespoon dried parsley
   2 teaspoons onion powder
   2 teaspoons garlic powder
   2 teaspoons dried oregano leaves
   2 teaspoons paprika
   2 teaspoons black pepper
1½ teaspoons salt
   4 pounds pork spareribs, cut into 4 racks
      Tennessee BBQ Sauce (recipe follows)

1. Combine chili powder, parsley, onion powder, garlic powder, oregano, paprika, pepper and salt in small bowl; mix well.

2. Rub spice mixture onto ribs. Cover; marinate in refrigerator at least 2 hours or overnight.

3. Preheat oven to 350°F. Place ribs in foil-lined shallow roasting pan. Bake 30 minutes.

4. Meanwhile, prepare grill for direct cooking. Prepare Tennessee BBQ sauce. Reserve 1 cup for dipping.

5. Place ribs on grid. Grill, covered, over medium heat 10 minutes. Brush with sauce. Continue grilling 10 minutes or until ribs are tender, brushing with sauce occasionally. Serve reserved sauce on the side for dipping.   *Makes 4 servings*

Tennessee BBQ Sauce

   3 cups prepared barbecue sauce
   ¼ cup cider vinegar
   ¼ cup honey
   2 teaspoons onion powder
   2 teaspoons garlic powder
      Dash hot pepper sauce

Combine all ingredients in medium bowl; mix well.
                                          Makes about 3½ cups

Memphis Pork Ribs

Chili Turkey Loaf

2 pounds ground turkey
1 cup chopped onion
⅔ cup Italian-style seasoned dry bread crumbs
½ cup chopped green bell pepper
½ cup chili sauce
2 eggs, lightly beaten
2 tablespoons horseradish mustard
4 cloves garlic, minced
1 teaspoon salt
½ teaspoon dried Italian seasoning
¼ teaspoon black pepper
    Prepared salsa (optional)

Slow Cooker Directions
Make foil handles for loaf using technique described below. Mix all ingredients except salsa in large bowl. Shape into round loaf and place on foil strips. Transfer to bottom of slow cooker using foil handles. Cover and cook on LOW 4½ to 5 hours or until juices run clear and temperature is 170°F. Remove loaf from slow cooker using foil handles. Place on serving plate. Let stand 5 minutes before serving. Cut into wedges and top with salsa, if desired. Serve with steamed carrots, if desired.   *Makes 8 servings*

Foil Handles: Tear off three 18×3-inch strips of heavy foil or use regular foil folded to double thickness. Crisscross foil strips in spoke design and place in slow cooker to allow for easy removal of turkey loaf.

Chili Turkey Loaf

Vermouth Salmon

2 (10×10-inch) sheets heavy-duty foil
2 salmon fillets or steaks (3 ounces each)
  Pinch of salt and black pepper
4 sprigs fresh dill
2 slices lemon
1 tablespoon vermouth

1. Preheat oven to 375°F. Turn up edges of 1 sheet of foil so juices will not run out. Place salmon in center of foil. Sprinkle with salt and pepper. Place dill and lemon slices on top of salmon. Pour vermouth evenly over fish pieces.

2. Cover fish with second sheet of foil. Crimp edges of foil together to seal packet leaving head space for heat circulation. Place packet on baking sheet. Bake 20 to 25 minutes or until salmon flakes easily when tested with fork. *Makes 2 servings*

Garlicky Chicken Packets

4 (12×12-inch) sheets heavy-duty foil
1 cup julienned carrots
½ cup sliced onion
¼ cup chopped fresh basil *or* 1 tablespoon dried basil leaves
2 tablespoons mayonnaise
6 cloves garlic, minced
⅛ teaspoon black pepper
4 boneless skinless chicken breast halves

1. Fold foil squares in half, then cut into shape of half hearts. Open foil to form hearts.

2. Preheat oven to 400°F. Place carrots and onion on 1 side of each heart near fold. Combine basil, mayonnaise, garlic and pepper in small bowl; spread mixture on chicken. Place chicken on top of vegetables. Fold foil over chicken; seal by creasing and folding edges of foil in small overlapping sections from top of heart until completed at point. Finish by twisting point and tucking under.

3. Place foil packages on ungreased baking sheet. Bake 20 to 25 minutes or until juices run clear and chicken is no longer pink in center. *Makes 4 servings*

Sausage, Potato and Apple Bake

3 tablespoons brown sugar
1 tablespoon dried thyme leaves
1 tablespoon dried oregano leaves
¼ cup dry white wine or apple cider
2 tablespoons cider vinegar
2 sweet potatoes (1½ to 2 pounds), peeled and cut into ¼-inch
   pieces
2 apples, such as Fuji or McIntosh, peeled, cored and cut into
   ¼-inch pieces
1 medium white onion, sliced into thin strips
1 red bell pepper, cut into thin strips
1 yellow bell pepper, cut into thin strips
½ cup golden raisins
4 sheets (18×12 inches) heavy-duty foil, lightly sprayed with
   nonstick cooking spray
1½ pounds smoked sausage, such as kielbasa or Polish sausage,
   sliced diagonally into ¼-inch pieces

1. Preheat oven to 450°F.

2. Combine brown sugar, thyme and oregano in large bowl. Stir in white wine and vinegar and stir until sugar is dissolved.

3. Add sweet potatoes, apples, onion, bell peppers and raisins; toss to coat. Using slotted spoon, divide potato mixture evenly among foil sheets. Fold up sides of foil around potato mixture.

4. Add sausage to bowl with remaining liquid; toss to coat. Divide sausage among four foil packets. Pour any remaining marinade over sausage mixture. Double fold sides and ends of foil to seal packets, leaving head space for heat circulation. Place packets on baking sheet.

5. Bake 20 minutes or until vegetables are tender. Remove packets from oven. Carefully open one end of each pack to allow steam to escape. Open packets and transfer contents to serving plates.

Makes 4 servings

Baked Salmon in Foil

2 tablespoons FILIPPO BERIO® Olive Oil, divided
1 (10-ounce) package frozen chopped spinach, thawed and
    squeezed dry
1 (8-ounce) can stewed tomatoes
1 onion, chopped
1 clove garlic, minced
4 salmon steaks, 1 inch thick (about 2 pounds)
4 pieces heavy-duty aluminum foil, each 12 inches square
4 thin lemon slices
1 tablespoon coarsely chopped fresh parsley
    Salt and freshly ground black pepper

Preheat oven to 375°F. In medium saucepan, heat 1 tablespoon olive oil over medium heat until hot. Add spinach, tomatoes, onion and garlic. Cook, stirring occasionally, 5 minutes or until mixture is thick and onion is tender.

In medium skillet, heat remaining 1 tablespoon olive oil over medium-high heat until hot. Add salmon; cook 1 to 2 minutes on each side or until lightly browned. Remove from heat. Place one-fourth of spinach mixture in center of each piece of foil; top with one salmon steak. Drizzle liquid from skillet over salmon. Top each with lemon slice and parsley. Fold edges of each foil square together. Pinch well to seal, completely enclosing filling. Place on baking sheet. Bake 15 minutes or until salmon flakes easily when tested with fork. To serve, cut an "X" on top of each packet; carefully peel back foil. Season to taste with salt and pepper. *Makes 4 servings*

Citrus Roasted Chicken

1 large foil cooking bag
1 tablespoon all-purpose flour
1 whole chicken (3 to 4 pounds)
½ cup chopped onion
2 tablespoons butter
  Juice of one lemon
  Juice of one lime
2 teaspoons grated lemon peel
¼ teaspoon salt
½ teaspoon dried thyme leaves
1 tablespoon fresh minced parsley

1. Preheat oven to 450°F. Place foil bag in 1-inch deep baking pan. Spray inside of bag with nonstick cooking spray. Dust with flour.

2. Rinse chicken and pat dry with paper towels. Remove and discard any excess fat. Place onion in chicken cavity and rub skin with butter. Place chicken in foil bag. Squeeze juice of lemon and lime over chicken. Sprinkle with grated lemon peel, salt and thyme. Seal foil bag.

3. Bake 1 hour or until juices run clear and thermometer inserted in thickest part of thigh registers 180°F. Remove from oven. Allow to cool 5 minutes before opening bag. Slit open top of bag to expose chicken; return to oven to brown skin, if desired. Garnish with fresh parsley and reserved juices. *Makes 6 servings*

Quick Tip: For more citrus flavor, add thinly sliced rounds of lemon and lime to the foil bag. The fruit will add more aroma as it cooks with the chicken.

That's Italian Meat Loaf

1 can (8 ounces) tomato sauce, divided
1 egg, lightly beaten
½ cup chopped onion
½ cup chopped green bell pepper
⅓ cup dry seasoned bread crumbs
2 tablespoons grated Parmesan cheese
½ teaspoon garlic powder
¼ teaspoon black pepper
1 pound ground beef
½ pound ground pork or veal
1 cup shredded Asiago cheese

Slow Cooker Directions

1. Reserve ⅓ cup tomato sauce; set aside in refrigerator. Combine remaining tomato sauce and egg in large bowl. Stir in onion, bell pepper, bread crumbs, Parmesan cheese, garlic powder and black pepper. Add ground beef and pork; mix well and shape into loaf.

2. Place meat loaf on foil strips (see tip). Place in slow cooker. Cover and cook on LOW 8 to 10 hours or on HIGH 4 to 6 hours; internal temperature should read 170°F.

3. Spread meat loaf with reserved tomato sauce. Sprinkle with Asiago cheese. Cover and cook 15 minutes or until cheese is melted. Using foil strips, remove meat loaf from slow cooker.   *Makes 8 servings*

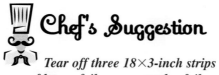 Chef's Suggestion

Tear off three 18×3-inch strips of heavy foil or use regular foil folded to double thickness. Crisscross foil strips in spoke design.

That's Italian Meat Loaf

Turkey Loaf with Quick Foil Potatoes

1 pound ground turkey breast (99% fat-free)
1¼ cups finely chopped onion, divided
½ cup finely chopped celery
2 eggs, beaten
6 tablespoons chili sauce, divided
1 clove garlic, minced
½ teaspoon salt
⅛ black pepper, plus more to taste
4 cups frozen shredded hash brown potatoes
1 to 2 tablespoons butter, cut into pieces

1. Preheat oven to 375°F. Line 8×8-inch baking pan with foil; lightly spray with nonstick cooking spray. Set aside.

2. Combine turkey, ¾ cup onion, celery, eggs, 5 tablespoons chili sauce, garlic, salt and ⅛ teaspoon pepper in large bowl; mix well. Form turkey mixture into loaf in foil-lined baking pan. Spread remaining 1 tablespoon chili sauce on top of loaf.

3. Bake 50 to 55 minutes until juices run clear and thermometer inserted in center of loaf registers 170°F.

4. Meanwhile, lightly spray 1 sheet (18×12 inches) heavy-duty foil with cooking spray. Combine frozen hash browns, remaining ½ cup onion and pepper to taste in medium bowl; mix well.

5. Place hash brown mixture in center of foil. Place butter on hash brown mixture. Double fold sides and ends of foil to seal packet. Place packet on small baking sheet.

6. When turkey loaf has baked for 20 minutes, place foil packet in oven. Bake on baking sheet 35 minutes. Remove turkey loaf and foil packet from oven. Let stand 5 minutes. Carefully open one end of foil packet to allow steam to escape. Open packet and transfer mixture to serving plates. Serve potatoes with sliced turkey loaf. *Makes 4 servings*

Vegetarian Orzo & Feta Bake

1 package (16 ounces) orzo pasta
1 can (4¼ ounces) chopped black olives, drained
2 cloves garlic, minced
1 sheet (24×18 inches) heavy-duty foil, lightly sprayed with
nonstick cooking spray
1 can (about 14 ounces) diced Italian-style tomatoes, undrained
1 can (14 ounces) vegetable broth
2 tablespoons olive oil
6 to 8 ounces feta cheese, cut into ½-inch cubes

1. Preheat oven to 450°F.

2. Combine orzo, olives and garlic in medium bowl. Place orzo mixture in center of foil sheet.

3. Fold sides of foil up around orzo mixture, but do not seal.

4. In same bowl, combine tomatoes with juices, broth and oil. Pour over orzo mixture. Top with cheese.

5. Double fold sides and ends of foil to seal packet, leaving head space for heat circulation. Place packet on baking sheet.

6. Bake 22 to 24 minutes or until pasta is tender. Remove from oven. Let stand 5 minutes. Open packet and transfer contents to serving plates.   *Makes 6 servings (or 8 side-dish servings)*

Citrus Chicken

4 boneless, skinless chicken breast halves
½ cup orange juice
2 tablespoons honey
2 tablespoons cornstarch
1 cup coarsely chopped onion
¼ teaspoon salt
⅛ teaspoon pepper
1 can (15 ounces) VEG-ALL® Original Mixed Vegetables, drained

Preheat oven to 375°F. Arrange chicken in a greased 8×8-inch square pan. In medium mixing bowl, combine orange juice, honey, and cornstarch. Add remaining ingredients and stir well. Pour over chicken and cover with foil. Bake for 30 to 35 minutes or until chicken is no longer pink in center. Place chicken on a bed of cooked rice. Pour sauce over chicken.   *Makes 4 servings*

Prep Time: 15 minutes
Cook Time: 35 minutes

Baked Fish with Fresh Mediterranean Salsa

4 lean, mild fish fillets (6 ounces each), such as flounder, tilapia or snapper
2 tablespoons water
½ teaspoon chili powder
1 large tomato, seeded and chopped
1 can (2½ ounces) sliced ripe olives or kalamata olives, drained
2 tablespoons chopped fresh parsley
2 tablespoons lemon juice
1 tablespoon capers, drained
2 teaspoons extra-virgin olive oil
1 teaspoon dried oregano leaves

1. Preheat oven to 350°F. Coat 12×8-inch glass baking dish with nonstick cooking spray; arrange fillets in single layer. Pour water over fillets and sprinkle with chili powder. Cover tightly with aluminum foil and bake 15 minutes or until fish is opaque in center.

2. Meanwhile, combine tomato, olives, parsley, lemon juice, capers, oil and oregano in small bowl; mix well. Remove fish from dish with slotted spatula and place on individual plates; spoon ⅓ cup salsa over each serving. *Makes 4 servings*

Chef's Suggestion

Capers are the small, pea-sized bud of a flower from the caper bush. Usually these green buds are pickled and can be found in the condiment section of the supermarket. They taste very much like gherkin pickles.

Baked Fish with Fresh Mediterranean Salsa

Country Roasted Chicken Dinner

1 envelope LIPTON® RECIPE SECRETS® Savory Herb with Garlic Soup Mix*
2 tablespoons honey
1 tablespoon water
1 tablespoon I CAN'T BELIEVE IT'S NOT BUTTER!® Spread, melted
1 roasting chicken (5 to 6 pounds)
3 pounds all-purpose and/or sweet potatoes, cut into chunks

*Also terrific with Lipton® Recipe Secrets® Golden Herb with Lemon or Golden Onion Soup Mix.

Preheat oven to 350°F.

In small bowl, blend savory herb with garlic soup mix, honey, water and I Can't Believe It's Not Butter!® Spread.

In 18×12-inch roasting pan, arrange chicken, breast side up; brush with soup mixture. Cover loosely with aluminum foil. Roast 30 minutes; drain off drippings. Arrange potatoes around chicken and continue roasting covered, stirring potatoes occasionally, 1 hour or until meat thermometer reaches 175°F and potatoes are tender. *If chicken reaches 175°F before potatoes are tender, remove chicken to serving platter and keep warm. Continue roasting potatoes until tender.*

Makes about 8 servings

Note: Insert meat thermometer into thickest part of thigh between breast and thigh; make sure tip does not touch bone.

Menu Suggestion: Serve with a mixed green salad, warm biscuits and Lipton® Iced Tea.

Chicken Baked in Foil

4 boneless skinless chicken breast halves (4 ounces each)
4 sheets (18×12) heavy-duty foil, lightly sprayed with nonstick
    cooking spray
1 cup matchstick-size carrot strips
1 cup matchstick-size zucchini strips
½ cup snow peas
½ cup thinly sliced red bell pepper
2¼ cups chicken broth, divided
2 tablespoons all-purpose flour
2 cloves garlic, minced
½ teaspoon dried thyme leaves
¼ teaspoon salt
¼ teaspoon ground nutmeg
¼ teaspoon black pepper
1 package (6 ounces) rice pilaf mix

1. Preheat oven to 375°F.

2. Place 1 chicken breast in center of each sheet of foil; arrange carrots, zucchini, peas and bell pepper around chicken.

3. Combine ½ cup chicken broth and flour in small saucepan; stir in garlic, thyme, salt, nutmeg and black pepper. Heat to a boil, stirring constantly, until thickened. Reduce heat to low; simmer 1 minute. Spoon broth mixture evenly over chicken and vegetables.

4. Double fold sides and edges of foil to seal packets, leaving head space for heat circulation. Place packets on baking sheet.

5. Bake 25 to 30 minutes or until chicken is not longer pink in center. Remove packets from oven. Carefully open one end of packets to allow steam to escape. Open packets and transfer contents to serving plates.

6. Meanwhile, place remaining 1¾ cups chicken broth in medium saucepan. Heat to a boil over medium-high heat. Stir in pilaf mix (discard spice packet). Reduce heat to low and simmer, covered, 15 minutes or until broth is absorbed. Serve with chicken.

Makes 4 servings

Fiesta Beef Enchiladas

6 ounces 90% lean ground beef
¼ cup sliced green onions
1 teaspoon fresh minced or bottled garlic
1 cup (4 ounces) shredded Mexican cheese blend or Cheddar
   cheese, divided
¾ cup chopped tomato, divided
½ cup frozen corn, thawed
⅓ cup cooked white or brown rice
¼ cup salsa or picante sauce
6 (6- to 7-inch) corn tortillas
2 sheets (20×12 inches) heavy-duty foil, generously sprayed
   with nonstick cooking spray
½ cup mild or hot red or green enchilada sauce
½ cup sliced romaine lettuce leaves

1. Preheat oven to 375°F.

2. Cook ground beef in medium nonstick skillet over medium heat until no longer pink; drain fat from skillet. Add green onions and garlic; cook and stir 2 minutes.

3. Combine meat mixture, ¾ cup cheese, ½ cup tomato, rice, corn and salsa; mix well. Spoon mixture down center of tortillas. Roll up; place, seam side down, on foil sheets, three to a sheet. Spoon enchilada sauce evenly over enchiladas.

4. Double fold sides and ends of foil to seal packets, leaving head space for heat circulation. Place packets on baking sheet.

5. Bake 15 minutes or until hot. Remove from oven; open packets. Sprinkle with remaining ¼ cup cheese; reseal packet. Bake 10 minutes more. Transfer contents to serving plates; serve with lettuce and remaining ¼ cup tomato.   *Makes 2 servings*

Prep Time: 15 minutes
Cook Time: 25 minutes

Golden Glazed Flank Steak

1 envelope LIPTON® RECIPE SECRETS® Onion Soup Mix*
1 jar (12 ounces) apricot or peach preserves
½ cup water
1 beef flank steak (about 2 pounds), cut into thin strips
2 medium green, red and/or yellow bell peppers, sliced
  Hot cooked rice

*Also terrific with LIPTON® RECIPE SECRETS® Onion-Mushroom Soup Mix.

1. In small bowl, combine soup mix, preserves and water; set aside.

2. On heavy-duty aluminum foil or in bottom of broiler pan with rack removed, arrange steak and green peppers; top with soup mixture.

3. Broil, turning steak and vegetables once, until steak is done. Serve over hot rice.   *Makes 8 servings*

 **Chef's Suggestion**

To make 3 cups hot cooked rice, combine 1 cup long-grain rice, 2 cups water, 1 teaspoon salt and 1 tablespoon oil in 3-quart saucepan. Cook over medium-high heat until water comes to a boil. Reduce heat to low; cover. Simmer until rice is tender, 15 to 20 minutes. Remove from heat; let stand 5 minutes. Uncover; fluff rice lightly with fork.

Golden Glazed Flank Steak

Citrus Grove Marinated Salmon

4 (6-ounce) salmon fillets or steaks
⅓ cup lemonade concentrate, thawed
¼ cup WESSON® Vegetable Oil
¼ cup orange juice concentrate, thawed
½ tablespoon fresh dill weed *or* ½ teaspoon dried dill weed
   PAM® No-Stick Cooking Spray

1. Rinse salmon and pat dry; set aside.

2. In small bowl, combine *remaining* ingredients *except* PAM Cooking Spray.

3. Place salmon in large resealable plastic food storage bag; pour ¾ marinade over fish; set *remaining* marinade aside. Seal bag and gently turn to coat; refrigerate 2 hours, turning fish several times during marinating.

4. Preheat broiler. Foil-line jelly-roll pan; spray with PAM Cooking Spray.

5. Place fish on pan; discard used marinade. Broil fish until it flakes easily with fork, basting frequently with *remaining* marinade.

Makes 4 (6-ounce) servings

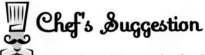

Chef's Suggestion

A member of the parsley family, dill weed is the dried soft feathery leaves of the dill plant. Its distinctive flavor can easily dominate a dish so you may want to use it sparingly at first.

Citrus Grove Marinated Salmon

Cheese-Stuffed Meatloaves

⅓ cup fine dry bread crumbs
2 ounces Cheddar cheese, cut into four 3×½×½-inch pieces
¾ cup ketchup
1 tablespoon all-purpose flour
1 tablespoon prepared mustard
1 egg, slightly beaten
¼ cup sliced green onions
½ teaspoon salt
¼ teaspoon black pepper
1 pound lean ground beef
1 large foil (17×15 inches) bag
2 tablespoons dill pickle relish

1. Preheat oven to 450°F. Place 1 tablespoon bread crumbs on sheet of wax paper. Set remaining bread crumbs aside. Roll cheese pieces in bread crumbs, pressing crumbs onto all sides. Set aside.

2. Combine ketchup, flour and mustard in small bowl. Set aside.

3. Combine egg, remaining bread crumbs, onions, 3 tablespoons ketchup mixture, salt and pepper in large bowl. Add ground beef; mix well. Form meat mixture into four individual (3½×2×1½-inch) meatloaves, shaping each loaf around piece of cheese. Completely enclose cheese with meat mixture.

4. Place foil bag in shallow baking pan. Spread half remaining ketchup mixture on center of one side of foil bag. Place meatloaves on top of ketchup mixture, leaving about 1-inch space between loaves. Spread remaining ketchup mixture over top of loaves.

5. Double fold open side of bag, leaving head space for heat circulation Bake 25 to 30 minutes or until internal temperature of loaves reaches 170°F. Carefully open bag and transfer meatloaves to serving plates. Sprinkle pickle relish on top of each meatloaf.   *Makes 4 servings*

Make-Ahead Dill Chicken in Foil

8 chicken thighs, skinned
1 teaspoon salt
½ teaspoon ground black pepper
½ cup butter or margarine, melted
2 tablespoons lemon juice
1 teaspoon dried dill weed
   Vegetable cooking spray
3 green onions, thinly sliced
1 cup thinly sliced carrots
6 ounces Swiss cheese, cut into 8 slices

Sprinkle chicken thighs with salt and pepper. Combine butter, lemon juice and dill in small bowl. Cut four 12-inch squares of heavy-duty foil; coat each with cooking spray. Place 1 tablespoon dill-butter sauce on center of each foil square; place 2 chicken thighs on sauce. Divide onion and carrot slices evenly over chicken. Top each with additional 1 tablespoon sauce and 1 slice cheese. Fold foil into packets, sealing securely. Label, date and freeze chicken until ready to bake.* To serve, place frozen foil packets in baking pan and bake at 400°F 1 hour or until fork can be inserted into chicken with ease and juices run clear, not pink. *Makes 4 servings*

Chicken may be frozen for up to 9 months. If serving immediately without freezing, place foil packets in baking pan and bake at 400°F 35 to 40 minutes or until fork can be inserted into chicken with ease and juices run clear, not pink.

Favorite recipe from *National Chicken Council*

Red Snapper Scampi

¼ cup butter or margarine, softened
1 tablespoon white wine
1½ teaspoons minced garlic
½ teaspoon grated lemon peel
⅛ teaspoon black pepper
4 red snapper, orange roughy or grouper fillets (about 4 to 5 ounces each)

1. Preheat oven to 450°F. Combine butter, wine, garlic, lemon peel and pepper in small bowl; stir to blend.

2. Place fish in foil-lined shallow baking pan. Top with seasoned butter. Bake 10 to 12 minutes or until fish begins to flake easily when tested with fork. *Makes 4 servings*

Prep and Cook Time: 12 minutes

 Chef's Suggestion

Serve fish over mixed salad greens, if desired. Or, add sliced carrots, zucchini and bell pepper cut into matchstick-size strips to the fish in the baking pan for an easy vegetable side dish.

Red Snapper Scampi

Magically Moist Chicken

1 pound boneless, skinless chicken breast halves
½ cup HELLMANN'S® or BEST FOODS® Real Mayonnaise
1¼ cups Italian seasoned dry bread crumbs

1. Preheat oven to 425°F. Brush chicken on all sides with mayonnaise.

2. In large plastic bag or bowl add bread crumbs. Add chicken, one piece at a time; toss to coat. On rack in broiler pan or on foil-lined baking sheet, arrange chicken.

3. Bake 20 minutes or until chicken is golden brown and thoroughly cooked.   *Makes 4 servings*

Prep Time: 5 minutes
Cook Time: 20 minutes

Magically Moist Chicken

Mediterranean Red Snapper

4 red snapper fillets (about 4 to 5 ounces each)
4 sheets (18×12 inches) heavy-duty foil, lightly sprayed with
nonstick cooking spray
8 sun-dried tomatoes, packed in oil, drained and chopped
⅓ cup sliced ripe olives
1½ teaspoons bottled minced garlic
½ teaspoon dried oregano leaves
½ teaspoon dried marjoram leaves
¼ teaspoon black pepper
⅛ teaspoon salt

1. Prepare grill for direct cooking.

2. Rinse snapper under cold running water; pat dry with paper towels. Place one fish fillet in center of one sheet of foil. Repeat with remaining fish and foil.

3. Combine tomatoes, olives, garlic, oregano, marjoram, pepper and salt. Sprinkle over fish.

4. Double-fold sides and ends of foil to seal packets, leaving head space for heat circulation. Place packets on baking sheet.

5. Slide packets off baking sheet onto grill grid. Grill, covered, over medium-high coals 9 to 11 minutes or until fish flakes with fork. Carefully open one end of each packet to allow steam to escape. Open packets and transfer mixture to serving plates.   *Makes 4 servings*

Buttermilk Oven-Fried Chicken

1½ cups buttermilk
4 teaspoons garlic powder, divided
2 teaspoons salt
2 teaspoons dried thyme leaves, divided
1 teaspoon dried sage
1 teaspoon paprika
½ teaspoon black pepper
2½ pounds chicken pieces, skin removed
   Nonstick cooking spray
1½ cups panko bread crumbs*
¼ cup all-purpose flour

Panko bread crumbs are light, crispy, Japanese-style bread crumbs. They can be found in the Asian aisle of most supermarkets. Unseasoned dry bread crumbs may be substituted.

1. Whisk buttermilk, 3 teaspoons garlic powder, 1 teaspoon thyme, salt, sage, paprika and pepper in large bowl until well blended. Add chicken; turn to coat. Cover and refrigerate at least 5 hours or overnight.

2. Preheat oven to 400°F. Line 2 baking sheets with foil; spray with cooking spray.

3. Combine bread crumbs, flour, remaining 1 teaspoon garlic powder and 1 teaspoon thyme in large shallow bowl. Remove chicken from buttermilk mixture, allowing excess to drip off. Coat chicken pieces one at a time with crumb mixture. Shake off excess crumbs. Place on prepared baking sheets; let stand 10 minutes.

4. Spray top portions of chicken with cooking spray. Bake about 50 minutes or until chicken is golden brown and juices run clear, turning once and spraying with additional cooking spray halfway through baking time.   *Makes about 8 servings*

One-Dish Creations

Chicken, Stuffing & Green Bean Bake

1 package (7 ounces) cubed herb-seasoned stuffing
4 sheets (18×12 inches) heavy-duty foil, lightly sprayed with
    nonstick cooking spray
½ cup chicken broth
3 cups frozen cut green beans
4 boneless skinless chicken breasts
1 cup chicken gravy
⅛ teaspoon black pepper
    Additional chicken gravy, heated (optional)

1. Preheat oven to 450°F.

2. Place a quarter of stuffing on one sheet of foil. Pour 2 tablespoons chicken broth over stuffing. Top stuffing with ¾ cup green beans. Place one chicken breast on top of beans. Combine gravy and pepper; pour ¼ cup over chicken.

3. Double fold sides and ends of foil to seal packet, leaving head space for heat circulation. Repeat with remaining stuffing, beans, chicken and gravy mixture to make three more packets. Place packets on baking sheet.

4. Bake 20 minutes or until chicken is no longer pink in center. Remove from oven. Carefully open one end of each packet to allow steam to escape. Open packets and transfer contents to serving plates. Serve with additional gravy, if desired.   *Makes 4 servings*

Chicken, Stuffing & Green Bean Bake

Asian Beef & Orange Packets

1 beef flank steak (about 1 pound)
2 cups uncooked instant rice
4 sheets (18×12 inches) heavy-duty foil, sprayed lightly with
 nonstick cooking spray
½ teaspoon black pepper
1 green bell pepper, cut into thin strips
1 red bell pepper, cut in thin strips
½ cup teriyaki sauce
¼ cup orange marmalade
1 can (11 ounces) mandarin orange sections, drained
8 ice cubes
1 cup beef broth or water
1 green onion, sliced (optional)

1. Preheat oven to 450°F.

2. Cut flank steak lengthwise in half, then crosswise into thin slices. Place ½ cup rice in center of one sheet of foil. Divide beef strips into four equal portions. Arrange four beef strips on foil to enclose rice and top with remainder of one portion of beef. Sprinkle with ⅛ teaspoon black pepper.

3. Place a quarter of bell peppers on beef. Combine teriyaki sauce and marmalade in small bowl. Drizzle 1 tablespoon teriyaki sauce mixture over vegetables.

4. Arrange a quarter of orange sections around beef and rice. Place 2 ice cubes on top of vegetables. Fold up sides of foil and pour ¼ cup broth into packet.

5. Double fold sides and ends of foil to seal packet, leaving head space for heat circulation. Repeat with remaining rice, beef, black pepper, bell peppers, sauce mixture, orange sections, ice cubes and broth to make three more packets. Place packets on baking sheet.

6. Bake 20 minutes or until beef and vegetables are tender. Remove from oven. Let stand 5 minutes. Open packets and transfer contents to serving plates. Garnish with green onion, if desired.

Makes 4 servings

Asian Beef & Orange Packets

Spicy Lasagna Rollers

1½ pounds Italian sausage, casings removed
1 jar (28 ounces) spaghetti sauce, divided
1 can (8 ounces) tomato sauce
½ cup chopped roasted red pepper
¾ teaspoon dried Italian seasoning
½ teaspoon red pepper flakes
1 container (15 ounces) ricotta cheese
1 package (10 ounces) frozen chopped spinach, thawed and squeezed dry
2 cups (8 ounces) shredded Italian cheese blend, divided
1 cup (4 ounces) shredded Cheddar cheese, divided
1 egg, lightly beaten
12 lasagna noodles, cooked and drained

1. Preheat oven to 350°F. Spray 13×9-inch baking pan with nonstick cooking spray; set aside.

2. Cook sausage in large skillet over medium heat until browned, stirring to break up meat; drain. Stir in ½ cup spaghetti sauce, tomato sauce, roasted pepper, Italian seasoning and pepper flakes.

3. Mix ricotta, spinach, 1½ cups Italian cheese blend, ½ cup Cheddar cheese and egg in medium bowl. Spread ¼ cup ricotta mixture over each noodle. Top with ⅓ cup sausage mixture. Tightly roll up each noodle from short end, jelly-roll style. Place rolls, seam sides down, in prepared pan. Pour remaining spaghetti sauce over rolls. Sprinkle with remaining ½ cup Italian cheese blend and ½ cup Cheddar cheese. Cover pan with foil.

4. Bake 30 minutes. Carefully remove foil; bake 15 minutes or until sauce is bubbly.

Makes 6 servings

Spicy Lasagna Rollers

Beefy Tostada Pie

2 teaspoons olive oil
1½ cups chopped onion
2 pounds ground beef
1 teaspoon chili powder
1 teaspoon ground cumin
1 teaspoon salt
2 cloves garlic, minced
1 can (15 ounces) tomato sauce
1 cup sliced black olives
8 flour tortillas
4 cups shredded Cheddar cheese
Sour cream, salsa and chopped green onion (optional)

Slow Cooker Directions

1. Heat oil in large skillet over medium heat. Add onion and cook until tender. Add ground beef, chili powder, cumin, salt and garlic; cook until browned. Stir in tomato sauce; heat through. Stir in black olives.

2. Make foil handles using three 18×2-inch strips of heavy foil. Crisscross foil to form spoke design. Place in slow cooker. Lay one tortilla on foil strips. Spread with meat sauce and layer of cheese. Top with another tortilla, meat sauce and cheese. Repeat layers ending with cheese. Cover and cook on HIGH 1½ hours. To serve, lift out of slow cooker using foil handles and transfer to serving platter. Discard foil. Cut into wedges. Serve with sour cream, salsa and chopped green onion, if desired. *Makes 4 to 5 servings*

Orange Roughy in Foil Hearts

4 sheets(12X12-inch) heavy-duty foil, lightly sprayed with
   nonstick cooking spray
4 orange roughy fillets (about 1½ pounds)
   Butter
8 ounces fresh asparagus, steamed and diagonally cut into
   2-inch pieces
1 yellow bell pepper, cut into 16 julienne strips
1 red bell pepper, cut into 16 julienne strips
1 medium carrot, cut into julienne strips
¼ cup dry white wine
3 tablespoons Dijon mustard
2 tablespoons lemon juice
1 teaspoon dried marjoram leaves
¼ teaspoon black pepper

Preheat oven to 375°F. Fold each foil square in half diagonally and cut into half heart shape.

Rinse orange roughy and pat dry with paper towels.

Lightly butter inside of each heart. Place 1 piece of fish on 1 side of each heart.

Divide asparagus; sprinkle over fish. Place 4 strips each yellow and red bell pepper over fish, then divide carrot strips over fish.

Combine wine, mustard, lemon juice, marjoram and black pepper in small bowl. Divide wine mixture over fish.

Fold foil hearts in half. Beginning at top of heart, fold the edges together, 2 inches at a time. At tip of heart, fold foil up and over.

Place hearts on large baking sheet. Bake 20 to 25 minutes or until fish flakes easily when tested with fork. To serve, place hearts on plates and cut an "X" through foil, folding points back to display contents.

Makes 4 servings

Mediterranean Chicken

4 boneless skinless chicken breasts
4 sheets (18×12 inches) heavy-duty foil, lightly sprayed with
    nonstick cooking spray
½ teaspoon dried oregano leaves
8 sun-dried tomatoes, cut into thin slivers
2 jars (6 ounces each) quartered marinated artichoke hearts,
    drained
1 can (about 4 ounces) sliced ripe olives, drained
2⅔ cups cubed unpeeled baking potatoes
¼ cup Parmesan and garlic salad dressing
    Chopped parsley (optional)

1. Preheat oven to 450°F.

2. Place one chicken breast in center of one sheet of foil. Sprinkle with
⅛ teaspoon oregano. Top with quarter of tomatoes, artichokes and
olives. Arrange ⅔ cup potatoes around the edge of chicken. Drizzle with
1 tablespoon salad dressing.

3. Double fold sides and ends of foil to seal packet, leaving head space
for heat circulation. Repeat with remaining chicken, oregano, vegetables
and dressing to make three more packets. Place packets on baking
sheet.

4. Bake 25 minutes or until chicken is no longer pink in center. Remove
packets from oven. Carefully open one end of each packet to allow
steam to escape. Open packets and transfer contents to serving plates.
Garnish, if desired, with chopped parsley.　　　　*Makes 4 servings*

Mile-High Enchilada Pie

8 (6-inch) corn tortillas
1 jar (12 ounces) prepared salsa
1 can (15½ ounces) kidney beans, rinsed and drained
1 cup shredded cooked chicken
1 cup shredded Monterey Jack cheese with jalapeño peppers

Slow Cooker Directions
Prepare foil handles for slow cooker (see below); place in slow cooker. Place 1 tortilla on bottom of slow cooker. Top with small amount of salsa, beans, chicken and cheese. Continue layering using remaining ingredients, ending with cheese. Cover; cook on LOW 6 to 8 hours or on HIGH 3 to 4 hours. Pull out by foil handles.

Makes 4 to 6 servings

Chef's Suggestion

To make foil handles, tear off three 18×3-inch strips of heavy foil or use regular foil folded to double thickness. Crisscross foil strips in spoke design and place in slow cooker to make lifting of tortilla stack easier.

Mile-High Enchilada Pie

Tilapia & Sweet Corn Baked in Foil

⅔ cup fresh or frozen corn kernels
¼ cup finely chopped onion
¼ cup finely chopped red bell pepper
2 cloves garlic, minced
1 teaspoon chopped fresh rosemary *or* ½ teaspoon crushed
    dried rosemary, divided
½ teaspoon salt, divided
¼ to ½ teaspoon black pepper, divided
2 sheets (18×12 inches) heavy-duty foil, lightly sprayed with
    nonstick cooking spray
2 tilapia fillets (4 ounces each)
1 teaspoon olive oil

1. Preheat toaster oven or oven to 400°F.

2. Combine corn, onion, bell pepper, garlic, ½ teaspoon fresh rosemary, ¼ teaspoon salt and half the black pepper in small bowl. Spoon half the corn mixture onto each sheet of foil, spreading out slightly.

3. Arrange tilapia fillets on top of corn mixture. Brush fish with oil; sprinkle with remaining ½ teaspoon fresh rosemary, ¼ teaspoon salt and black pepper.

4. Double fold sides and ends of foil to seal packets, leaving head space for heat circulation. Place packets on toaster oven tray or on baking sheet.

5. Bake 15 minutes or until fish is opaque throughout. Remove packets from oven. Carefully open one end of each packet to allow steam to escape. Open packets and transfer contents to serving plates.

Makes 2 servings

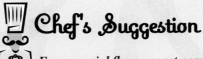 **Chef's Suggestion**

For a special flavor, roast corn and red bell pepper on foil-lined baking sheet, lightly sprayed with nonstick cooking spray, in 450°F oven for 15 minutes or until slightly brown, stirring once. Then proceed with recipe as directed above.

Barbara's Pork Chop Dinner

Nonstick cooking spray
6 bone-in pork loin chops (¾ inch thick)
1 small onion, thinly sliced and separated into rings
6 sheets (18×12 inches) heavy-duty foil, lightly sprayed with nonstick cooking spray
6 medium red potatoes, unpeeled and cut into thin slices
1 can (10¾ ounces) condensed cream of chicken soup, undiluted
1 cup sliced fresh mushrooms
⅓ cup canned chicken broth
2 tablespoons Dijon mustard
2 cloves garlic, minced
½ teaspoon salt
½ teaspoon dried basil leaves
¼ teaspoon black pepper
Chopped fresh parsley

1. Preheat oven to 450°F.

2. Spray large nonstick skillet with cooking spray. Brown pork chops quickly on both sides. Set aside.

3. Divide onion rings into 6 portions. Place one portion of onion rings on each sheet of foil. Top with potato slices.

4. Combine soup, mushrooms, chicken broth, mustard, mushrooms, garlic, salt, basil and pepper in medium bowl. Pour some soup mixture over potatoes and onion. Top with pork chops and remaining soup mixture.

5. Double fold sides and ends of foil to seal packets, leaving head space for heat circulation. Place packets on baking sheet.

6. Bake 28 to 30 minutes or until potatoes are tender. Remove packets from oven. Carefully open one end of each packet to allow steam to escape. Open packets and transfer contents to serving plates. Sprinkle with parsley.   *Makes 6 servings*

Chicken and Veggie Lasagna

Tomato-Herb Sauce with Chicken (recipe follows)
Nonstick olive oil cooking spray
1½ cups thinly sliced zucchini
1 cup thinly sliced carrots
3 cups torn fresh spinach leaves
½ teaspoon salt
1 package (15 ounces) fat-free ricotta cheese
½ cup grated Parmesan cheese
9 lasagna noodles, cooked and drained
2 cups (8 ounces) reduced-fat shredded mozzarella cheese

1. Prepare Tomato-Herb Sauce.

2. Preheat oven to 350°F. Spray large nonstick skillet with cooking spray; heat over medium heat until hot. Add zucchini and carrots; cook and stir about 5 minutes or until almost tender. Remove from heat; stir in spinach and salt.

3. Combine ricotta and Parmesan cheese in small bowl. Spread 1⅔ cups Tomato-Herb Sauce on bottom of 13×9-inch baking pan. Top with 3 noodles. Spoon half of ricotta cheese mixture over noodles; spread lightly with spatula. Spoon half of zucchini mixture over ricotta cheese mixture; sprinkle with 1 cup mozzarella cheese. Repeat layers; place remaining 3 noodles on top.

4. Spread remaining Tomato-Herb Sauce over noodles. Cover with aluminum foil; bake 1 hour or until sauce is bubbly. Let stand 5 to 10 minutes; cut into rectangles. Garnish as desired. *Makes 12 servings*

Tomato-Herb Sauce with Chicken

Nonstick olive oil cooking spray
1½ cups chopped onions (about 2 medium)
4 cloves garlic, minced
1 tablespoon dried basil leaves
1 teaspoon dried oregano leaves
½ teaspoon dried tarragon leaves
¼ teaspoon dried thyme leaves
2½ pounds ripe tomatoes, peeled and cut into wedges
1 pound ground chicken, cooked, crumbled and drained
¼ cup no-salt-added tomato paste
½ teaspoon *each* salt and black pepper

continued on page 72

Chicken and Veggie Lasagna

1. Spray large nonstick skillet with cooking spray; heat over medium heat until hot. Add onions, garlic, basil, oregano, tarragon and thyme; cook and stir about 5 minutes or until onions are tender.

2. Add tomatoes, chicken, ¾ cup water and tomato paste; heat to a boil. Reduce heat to low and simmer, uncovered, about 20 minutes or until sauce is reduced to 5 cups. Stir in salt and pepper.　　*Makes 5 cups*

Steak & Gnocchi Bake

 2 packages (1 pound each) gnocchi (frozen or dried)
 ½ pound button mushrooms
 1 boneless beef top sirloin steak (1½ to 2 pounds)
    Salt
    Black pepper
 ½ cup steak sauce
 ¼ to ⅓ cup grated Parmesan cheese
 3 tablespoons butter, softened to room temperature
 3 tablespoons whole-grain mustard
 6 to 8 sheets (18×12 inches) heavy-duty foil, lightly sprayed
    with nonstick cooking spray

1. Preheat oven to 450°F. Cook gnocchi according to package directions; drain.

2. Gently combine prepared gnocchi and mushrooms in medium bowl.

3. Cut steak across the grain into ⅛-inch slices. Season to taste with salt and pepper.

4. Combine steak sauce, cheese, butter and mustard in small bowl.

5. Place one-sixth gnocchi mixture in center of each sheet of foil. Divide beef into six portions and arrange on top of gnocchi mixture. Divide sauce mixture into six portions and place on beef.

6. Double fold sides and ends of foil to seal packets, leaving head space for heat to circulation. Place packets on baking sheet.

7. Bake 12 to 15 minutes until beef is tender. Remove packets from oven. Carefully open one end of each packet to allow steam to escape. Open packets and transfer contents to serving plates.

Makes 6 to 8 servings

Chicken and Sausage Jambalaya

6 sheets (15×12 inches) heavy-duty foil, lightly sprayed with nonstick cooking spray
2 cups uncooked instant rice
12 ounces chicken breasts, cut into thin strips
12 ounces Italian sausage, casings removed, cut into ½-inch slices
1 can (28 ounces) diced tomatoes, drained
1 can (8 ounces) tomato sauce
1 green bell pepper, finely diced
1 medium onion, chopped
1 teaspoon dried thyme
1 teaspoon salt
½ teaspoon black pepper
⅛ to ¼ teaspoon ground red pepper

1. Preheat oven to 450°F.

2. Place ⅓ cup rice in center of one sheet of foil. Divide chicken strips into six equal portions. Arrange 5 to 6 chicken strips on foil to enclose. Top with remainder of one portion of chicken. Top rice with ⅙ of sausage.

3. Combine tomatoes, tomato sauce, bell pepper, onion, thyme, salt, black pepper and red pepper in medium bowl. Place ½ cup sauce mixture over sausage and rice.

4. Place 3 ice cubes on rice mixture. Double fold sides and ends of foil to seal packet, leaving head space for heat circulation. Repeat with remaining rice, chicken, sausage, sauce mixture and ice cubes to make 5 more packets. Place bags 1 inch apart on baking sheets.

5. Bake 20 to 22 minutes or until chicken and sausage are cooked through. Let stand 10 minutes. Open packets and place on individual serving plates. *Makes 6 servings*

Tamale Pies

  1 pound ground pork, beef or turkey
  1 tablespoon chili powder
  2 cloves garlic, minced
  ½ teaspoon salt
  1 cup shredded Monterey-Jack cheese
  1 package (8½ ounces) corn bread mix, plus ingredients to
     prepare mix
  1 can (11 ounces) Mexican-style whole kernel corn, drained
  6 sheets (12×12 inches) heavy-duty foil, lightly sprayed with
     nonstick cooking spray
 12 tablespoons mild or hot salsa
  4 tablespoons regular or fat-free sour cream
  6 cilantro sprigs (optional)

1. Preheat oven to 450°F.

2. Combine pork, chili powder, garlic and salt in nonstick skillet. Cook over medium-high heat, stirring to break up lumps, until pork is no longer pink and moisture has evaporated. Remove from heat; stir in cheese. Set aside.

3. Prepare corn bread mix according to package directions. Stir in corn.

4. Place about ½ cup pork mixture in center of one foil sheet; flatten slightly. Top with ¼ cup corn bread mix. Spread lightly over pork. (It is not necessary to cover sides of pork.) Double fold sides and ends of foil to seal packet, leaving head space for heat circulation. Repeat with remaining pork mixture, corn bread mix and foil to make 5 more packets. Place packets on baking sheet.

5. Bake 12 minutes. Let stand 5 minutes. Carefully open packets and transfer contents to serving plates. Garnish each pie with 2 tablespoons salsa, 2 teaspoons sour cream and cilantro sprig, if desired.

Makes 6 servings

Tamale Pie

Chicken with Cornbread Dumplings

4 boneless skinless chicken breasts (about 1 to 1½ pounds)
½ cup chicken broth
½ cup half-and-half
1 teaspoon salt
1 teaspoon dried thyme leaves
1 teaspoon black pepper
½ teaspoon dried sage leaves
1 red bell pepper, diced
1 can (8 ounces) cut green beans *or* 1 package (9 ounces) cut
**   green beans, thawed and drained**
1 can (8 ounces) corn, drained
4 sheets (12×12 inches) heavy-duty foil, lightly sprayed with
**   nonstick cooking spray**
1 can (11½ ounces) refrigerated cornbread twists

1. Preheat oven to 450°F. Cut chicken breasts into ¾-inch cubes.

2. Mix chicken broth, half-and-half, salt, thyme, pepper and sage in large bowl. Add chicken, bell pepper, green beans and corn; stir to coat. Divide mixture evenly among four sheets of foil, reserving liquid. Fold up sides of foil around chicken mixture, but do not seal.

3. Cut cornbread twists into pieces about 1 inch long; divide evenly among packets, placing cornbread pieces around outside edge of chicken mixture.

4. Adjust foil around chicken mixture, if necessary, leaving tops of packets open. Pour reserved liquid into foil packets, about 3 tablespoons per packet. Double fold sides and ends of foil to seal packets, leaving head space for heat circulation. Place packets on baking sheet.

5. Bake 18 to 24 minutes or until chicken is no longer pink. Remove from oven. Carefully open one end of packets to allow steam to escape. Open packets and transfer contents to serving plates.

Makes 4 servings

Note: One (7-ounce) cornbread mix, prepared according to package directions, may be substituted for the refrigerated cornbread twists. Drop by rounded teaspoonfuls around edges of chicken mixture.

Tuscan Steak and Beans

⅓ cup balsamic vinegar
3 cloves garlic, minced
2¼ pounds boneless top loin sirloin steak, cut into six 6-ounce
   steaks
1 tablespoon dried oregano leaves
6 sheets (15×12 inches) heavy-duty foil, lightly sprayed with
   nonstick cooking spray
1 package (16 ounces) frozen lima beans
1 package (8 ounces) sliced mushrooms
1½ teaspoons salt
1½ teaspoons black pepper
1 lemon, cut lengthwise into 6 wedges

1. Preheat oven to 450°F.

2. Combine vinegar and garlic in large resealable plastic food storage bag; add steaks. Seal bag; turn to coat steaks.

3. Remove steaks from marinade; discard remaining marinade. Sprinkle ½ teaspoon oregano in center of one foil sheet. Lay 1 steak on top. Spoon about ½ cup lima beans over half of steak. Sprinkle about ½ cup sliced mushrooms over other half of steak. Sprinkle steak and vegetables with ¼ teaspoon salt and ¼ teaspoon pepper. Double fold sides and ends of foil to seal packet, leaving head space for heat circulation. Repeat with remaining oregano, steaks, lima beans, mushrooms, salt and pepper. Place packets on baking sheet.

4. Bake 25 to 30 minutes. Let stand 5 minutes. Carefully open packets and transfer contents to serving plates. Top each steak with lemon wedge. *Makes 6 servings*

Note: Steaks can be prepared on grill. Prepare grill for direct cooking. Continue as directed above. Grill, covered, 16 minutes.

Quick Beef Stew in Foil

8 ounces boneless beef top sirloin steak, cut into 1-inch cubes
1 medium red potato, peeled and cut into ¾-inch cubes
1 cup frozen mixed vegetables
⅔ cup beef gravy
½ teaspoon parsley flakes
¼ teaspoon salt
¼ teaspoon dried thyme leaves
⅛ teaspoon black pepper
1 sheet (20×12 inches) heavy-duty foil, lightly sprayed with
    nonstick cooking spray

1. Preheat oven to 450°F.

2. Combine all ingredients except foil in medium bowl; stir to mix.

3. Place beef mixture in center of foil sheet. Double fold sides and ends of foil to seal packet, leaving head space for heat circulation. Place packet on baking sheet.

4. Bake 30 minutes or until beef is tender. Carefully open one end of packet to allow steam to escape. Open packet and transfer stew to two bowls.   *Makes 2 servings*

Foil Baked Albacore

½ cup frozen peas
½ cup sliced carrot
½ cup sliced red or green bell pepper or zucchini
⅓ cup sliced onion
2 large mushrooms, sliced
1 (3-ounce) pouch of STARKIST® Premium Albacore Tuna
¼ cup bottled Italian dressing
    Salt and pepper to taste
1 large tomato, quartered
⅓ cup shredded Cheddar cheese (optional)

Combine vegetables; divide between 2 pieces (each 12 inches square) of heavy-duty foil. Divide tuna in half; mound over vegetables. Drizzle each serving with dressing; add salt and pepper. Add 2 tomato quarters to each serving; sprinkle with cheese, if desired. Fold foil into closed packet, sealing edges securely. Bake in 450°F oven 15 minutes or cook on barbecue until thoroughly heated.   *Makes 2 servings*

Prep Time: 25 minutes

Layered Mexican-Style Casserole

2 cans (15½ ounces each) hominy*, drained
1 can (15 ounces) black beans, rinsed and drained
1 can (14½ ounces) diced tomatoes with garlic, basil and
    oregano, undrained
1 cup thick and chunky salsa
1 can (6 ounces) tomato paste
½ teaspoon ground cumin
3 large (about 9-inch diameter) flour tortillas
2 cups (8 ounces) shredded Monterey Jack cheese
¼ cup sliced black olives

*Hominy is corn that has been treated with slaked lime to remove the germ and hull. It can be found with the canned vegetables in most supermarkets.

Slow Cooker Directions

1. Prepare foil handles (see below). Spray with nonstick cooking spray.

2. Stir together hominy, beans, tomatoes with juice, salsa, tomato paste and cumin in large bowl.

3. Press one tortilla in bottom of slow cooker. (Edges of tortilla may turn up slightly.) Top with one third of hominy mixture and one third of cheese. Repeat layers. Press remaining tortilla on top. Top with remaining hominy mixture. Set aside remaining cheese.

4. Cover; cook on LOW 6 to 8 hours. Sprinkle with remaining cheese and olives. Cover; let stand 5 minutes. Pull out tortilla stack with foil handles.   *Makes 6 servings*

Foil Handles: Tear off three 18×3-inch strips of heavy-duty foil or use regular foil folded to double thickness. Crisscross foil strips in spoke design and place into slow cooker to make lifting of tortilla stack easier.

Prep Time: 10 minutes
Cook Time: 6 to 8 hours
Stand Time: 5 minutes

Layered Mexican-Style Casserole

Apricot Pork Chops and Dressing

1 box (6 ounces) herb-seasoned stuffing mix
½ cup dried apricots (about 16), cut into quarters
6 sheets (18×12-inches) heavy-duty foil, lightly sprayed with
nonstick cooking spray
6 bone-in pork chops, ½ inch thick
Salt
Black pepper
6 tablespoons apricot jam
1 bag (16 ounces) frozen green peas
3 cups matchstick carrots*

*Precut matchstick carrots are available in the produce section of large supermarkets.

1. Preheat oven to 450°F. Prepare stuffing mix according to package directions; stir in apricots.

2. Place ½ cup stuffing mixture in center of one sheet of foil. Place 1 pork chop over stuffing mixture, pressing down slightly and shaping stuffing to conform to shape of chop. Sprinkle chop with salt and pepper. Spread 1 tablespoon apricot jam over pork chop.

3. Place ⅔ cup peas beside pork chop in curve of bone. Arrange ½ cup carrots around outside of chop.

4. Double fold sides and ends of foil to seal packet, leaving head space for heat circulation. Repeat with remaining stuffing mixture, pork chops, salt, pepper, jam and vegetables to make 5 more packets. Place packets on baking sheet.

5. Bake 25 minutes or until pork chops are barely pink in centers and vegetables are tender. Remove from oven. Carefully open one end of each packet to allow steam to escape. Open packets and transfer contents to serving plates. *Makes 6 servings*

Apricot Pork Chop and Dressing

Honey-Mustard Chicken with Sauerkraut & Spuds

2 tablespoons stone-ground mustard
1 tablespoon honey
2 boneless skinless chicken breasts
2 medium red potatoes, thinly sliced
2 sheets (18×12 inches) heavy-duty foil, lightly sprayed with nonstick cooking spray
¼ teaspoon salt
⅛ teaspoon black pepper
1½ cups fresh sauerkraut, divided
2 slices Swiss cheese
2 teaspoons minced fresh parsley *or* 1 teaspoon dried parsley flakes
Additional mustard

1. Preheat toaster oven or oven to 450°F.

2. Combine mustard and honey in medium bowl. Add chicken and turn several times to coat with mustard mixture. Let stand 10 minutes.

3. Meanwhile, divide potato slices between foil sheets, overlapping slices to form a rectangle about size of chicken breast. Sprinkle potato slices with salt and pepper.

4. Place chicken on potato slices. Top with sauerkraut and cheese slices. Sprinkle with parsley.

5. Double fold sides and ends of foil to seal packets, leaving head space for heat circulation. Place packets on toaster oven tray or baking sheet. Bake 35 to 40 minutes or until chicken is no longer pink in center and potatoes are tender.

6. Remove packets from oven. Carefully open one end of packets to allow steam to escape. Open packets and transfer contents to serving plates. Serve with additional mustard. *Makes 2 servings*

Orange Teriyaki Pork Packets

½ **pound lean cubed pork stew meat (1-inch cubes)**
2 **sheets (18×12 inches) heavy-duty foil, lightly sprayed with**
   nonstick cooking spray
1½ **cups frozen pepper blend for stir-fry**
¼ **cup water chestnuts, coarsely chopped**
1 **tablespoon cornstarch**
2 **tablespoons teriyaki sauce**
2 **tablespoons orange marmalade**
¼ **teaspoon ground ginger**
½ **teaspoon dry mustard**
   Hot cooked rice

1. Preheat oven to 450°F.

2. Combine pork, pepper blend and water chestnuts in medium bowl; toss to mix. Place half of mixture on each foil sheet.

3. Dissolve cornstarch in teriyaki sauce. Stir in marmalade, ginger and mustard. Pour mixture over pork and vegetables.

4. Double fold sides and ends of foil to seal packets, leaving head space for heat circulation. Place packets on baking sheet.

5. Bake 20 to 23 minutes or until pork is tender. Remove from oven. Carefully open one end of each packet to allow steam to escape. Open packets and transfer contents to serving plates. Serve with rice.

Makes 2 servings

Moroccan-Style Chicken and Couscous

1½ cups water
⅓ cup raisins
2 chicken bouillon cubes
2 tablespoons olive oil or butter
1 cup quick-cooking couscous
4 boneless skinless chicken breasts (about 6 ounces each)
    flattened to ¼-inch thick
4 teaspoons mild curry powder
4 sheets (18×12 inches) heavy-duty foil, lightly sprayed with
    nonstick cooking spray
Sweet Lemon Sauce (recipe follows) or prepared mango
    chutney

1. Preheat oven to 450°F.

2. Bring water, raisins, bouillon cubes and olive oil to a boil in 2-quart saucepan. Add couscous; stir; cover and remove from heat. Let stand 5 minutes; fluff with fork.

3. Place ½ cup couscous in center of one sheet of foil. Dust one chicken breast on both sides with 1 teaspoon curry powder. Shape chicken around stuffing. Double fold sides and ends to seal, leaving head space for heat circulation. Repeat with remaining foil, couscous, chicken and curry.

4. Place packets on baking sheet. Bake 20 minutes.

5. Meanwhile, prepare Sweet Lemon Sauce.

6. Remove packets from oven. Let stand 5 minutes. Open packets and carefully transfer contents to serving plates. Serve with Sweet Lemon Sauce or prepared mango chutney.   *Makes 4 servings*

Sweet Lemon Sauce

1 lemon
½ cup plus 2 teaspoons honey, divided
½ cup water

1. Cut lemon into thin slices, discarding ends. Remove and discard seeds.

2. Place lemon, ½ cup honey and water in small saucepan. Bring to a boil, stirring frequently.

3. Add remaining 2 tablespoon honey; stir and cover. Remove from heat until ready to serve.   *Makes about 1 cup*

Moroccan-Style Chicken and Couscous

Steak San Marino

¼ cup all-purpose flour
1 teaspoon salt
½ teaspoon black pepper
1¼ pounds boneless beef top sirloin steak, cut into 4 pieces
4 sheets (18×12 inches) heavy-duty foil, lightly sprayed with
    nonstick cooking spray
1 can (8 ounces) tomato sauce
1 carrot, chopped
½ onion, chopped
1 rib celery, chopped
1 teaspoon dried Italian seasoning
½ teaspoon Worcestershire sauce
Hot cooked rice

1. Preheat oven to 450°F.

2. Combine flour, salt and pepper in small bowl. Coat beef in flour mixture. Place each piece of beef on foil. Combine tomato sauce, carrot, onion, celery, Italian seasoning and Worcestershire sauce in small bowl; pour a quarter of tomato sauce mixture over each piece of beef.

3. Double fold sides and ends of foil to seal packets, leaving head space for heat circulation. Place packets on baking sheet.

4. Bake 25 to 28 minutes or until beef is tender. Remove packets from oven. Carefully open one end of each packet to allow steam to escape. Open packets and transfer contents to serving plates. Serve steaks and sauce over rice.   *Makes 4 servings*

Chicken Divan

1 cup uncooked instant rice
2 sheets (18×12 inches) heavy-duty foil, lightly sprayed with nonstick cooking spray
8 chicken tenders*
1½ cups broccoli florets
¼ cup chicken broth
4 ice cubes
⅔ cup Alfredo pasta sauce
2 tablespoons grated Parmesan cheese

*Or, substitute two chicken breast halves for chicken tenders.

1. Preheat oven to 450°F.

2. Place ½ cup rice in center of one sheet of foil. Place 4 chicken tenders on foil to enclose rice. Arrange half of broccoli on chicken. Pour 2 tablespoons chicken broth over rice. Top with two ice cubes.

3. Pour ⅓ cup sauce over chicken and broccoli. Sprinkle with 1 tablespoon cheese.

4. Double fold sides and ends of foil to seal packet, leaving head space for heat circulation. Repeat with remaining rice, chicken, broccoli, broth, ice cubes, sauce and cheese. Place packets on baking sheet.

5. Bake 15 minutes or until chicken is no longer pink in center. Remove from oven. Let stand 5 minutes. Carefully, open packets and transfer contents to serving plates. *Makes 2 servings*

Oven Roasted Pork & "Two" Potatoes

¾ cup LAWRY'S® Herb & Garlic Marinade with Lemon Juice,
   divided
1 teaspoon dried thyme
2 pounds pork tenderloin
1 tablespoon BERTOLLI® Olive Oil
½ pound sweet potatoes or yams, peeled and diagonally sliced
   ½-inch thick
¾ pound red potatoes, unpeeled and cut into 2-inch chunks
1 large onion, peeled and sliced into 1-inch wedges

In small bowl, mix together Herb & Garlic Marinade and thyme;
reserve ¼ cup of mixture. Pierce pork deeply with fork in several
places. In large resealable plastic bag, add ¼ cup of marinade mixture
and pork; seal bag. Marinate in refrigerator for 30 minutes. Remove
pork from bag, discarding used marinade. In large bowl or another large
resealable plastic bag, combine oil, sweet potatoes, red potatoes, onion
and ¼ cup of marinade mixture; toss to coat. On bottom of foil lined
broiler pan, place pork in center and surround with potato mixture.
Roast in preheated 450°F oven for 20 minutes. Brush pork and potatoes
with remaining ¼ cup of marinade mixture, turning pork over to brush.
Return pan to oven and continue roasting until pork reaches internal
temperature of 150°F, about 15 to 20 minutes longer.

Makes 4 to 6 servings

Prep. Time: 12 to 15 minutes
Marinate Time: 30 minutes
Cook Time: 35 to 40 minutes

Oven Roasted Pork & "Two" Potatoes

Stuffed Bell Pepper

½ cup chopped fresh tomatoes
1 teaspoon chopped fresh cilantro (optional)
½ clove garlic, minced
¼ teaspoon dried oregano leaves
⅛ teaspoon ground cumin
4 ounces lean ground round
¼ cup cooked brown or white rice
2 tablespoons cholesterol-free egg substitute *or* 1 egg white
1 tablespoon finely chopped onion
⅛ teaspoon salt
⅛ teaspoon black pepper
1 large bell pepper, any color, seeded and cut in half lengthwise
2 sheets (12×12 inches) heavy-duty foil, lightly sprayed with
     nonstick cooking spray

1. Preheat toaster oven or oven to 400°F.

2. Combine tomatoes, cilantro, if desired, garlic, oregano and cumin in small bowl. Set aside.

3. Thoroughly combine beef, rice, egg substitute, onion, salt and black pepper in medium bowl. Stir ⅓ cup tomato mixture into beef mixture. Spoon filling evenly into pepper halves; place each pepper half on foil sheet.

4. Double fold sides and ends of foil to seal packet. Place on toaster oven tray (or baking sheet if using oven).

5. Bake 30 minutes or until beef is no longer pink and pepper halves are tender. Serve with remaining tomato salsa, if desired.

Makes 2 servings

Old World Chicken and Vegetables

¾ teaspoon dried oregano leaves, divided
½ teaspoon paprika
¼ teaspoon salt
¼ teaspoon garlic powder
⅛ teaspoon black pepper
2 skinless bone-in chicken breasts
2 sheets (18×12) heavy-duty foil, lightly sprayed with nonstick
   cooking spray
½ cup pasta sauce
½ medium green bell pepper, cut into squares
½ cup chopped mushrooms
¼ cup chopped onion
   Parmesan cheese
   Hot cooked egg noodles

1. Preheat toaster oven or oven to 450°F. Combine ½ teaspoon oregano, paprika, salt, garlic powder and black pepper in small bowl; mix well.

2. Place chicken on foil sheets. Sprinkle each chicken breasts with half oregano mixture. Combine pasta sauce, bell pepper, mushrooms, onion and remaining ¼ teaspoon oregano in medium bowl. Pour half of sauce mixture over each chicken breast.

3. Double fold sides and ends of foil to seal packets, leaving head space for heat circulation. Place packets on toaster oven tray (or baking sheet if using oven).

4. Bake 23 to 25 minutes or until chicken juices run clear. Carefully open ends of packets to allow steam to escape. Open packets and transfer contents to serving plates. Sprinkle with Parmesan cheese. Serve with noodles. *Makes 2 servings*

Summer Vegetable & Fish Bundles

4 fish fillets (about 1 pound)
1 pound thinly sliced vegetables*
1 envelope LIPTON® RECIPE SECRETS® Savory Herb with Garlic
   or Golden Onion Soup Mix
½ cup water

Use any combination of the following: thinly sliced mushrooms, zucchini, yellow squash or tomatoes.

On two 18×18-inch pieces heavy-duty aluminum foil, divide fish equally; top with vegetables. Evenly pour savory herb with garlic soup mix blended with water over fish. Wrap foil loosely around fillets and vegetables, sealing edges airtight with double fold. Grill or broil, seam side up, 15 minutes or until fish flakes easily with fork.

Makes 4 servings

Chef's Suggestion

Serve over hot cooked rice with Lipton® Iced Tea mixed with a splash of cranberry juice cocktail.

Carmel Chicken Fresco Bake

4 cups broccoli florets
4 tablespoons butter, divided
12 ounces baby portobello mushrooms, sliced
3 shallots, diced
1 can (14 ounces) artichoke hearts, rinsed, drained and
  quartered
4 tablespoons all-purpose flour
2½ cups chicken broth
1 teaspoon Dijon mustard
½ teaspoon salt
½ teaspoon dried tarragon leaves
½ teaspoon black pepper
1 cup (4 ounces) shredded Emmentaler cheese
2 pounds boneless skinless chicken breasts, cooked and cut
  into 1½-inch cubes
¼ cup grated Asiago cheese

1. Preheat oven to 350°F. Spray 4-quart baking dish with nonstick cooking spray; set aside.

2. Steam broccoli about 6 minutes or until tender. Rinse and drain under cold water. Set aside.

3. Melt 1 tablespoon butter in medium skillet over medium heat. Add mushrooms and shallots; cook and stir about 5 minutes or until soft. Remove from skillet and combine with broccoli in large bowl. Stir in artichoke hearts.

4. Melt remaining 3 tablespoons butter in same skillet. Blend in flour. Add chicken broth, mustard, salt, tarragon and pepper; whisk about 2 minutes or until sauce thickens. Add Emmentaler cheese and stir until smooth.

5. Alternately layer chicken and vegetable mixture in baking dish. Pour cheese sauce over top of casserole. Cover with foil and bake 40 minutes. Remove foil; sprinkle with Asiago cheese. Bake 5 to 10 minutes. *Makes 8 servings*

Spinach-Stuffed Roulade

1 pound ground beef
1 pound Italian sausage, casings removed and crumbled
1½ cups seasoned bread crumbs
2 eggs, lightly beaten
2 tablespoons chopped fresh parsley
2 cloves garlic, minced
1 teaspoon salt
½ teaspoon black pepper
2 cups water
1 tablespoon butter
1 package (about 4 ounces) Spanish rice mix
2 packages (10 ounces each) frozen chopped spinach, thawed
  and well drained

1. Combine ground beef, sausage, bread crumbs, eggs, parsley, garlic, salt and pepper in large bowl; mix well. Place on 12×12-inch sheet of foil moistened with water. Cover with 12×14-inch sheet of waxed paper moistened with water. With hands or rolling pin, press meat mixture into 12×12-inch rectangle. Refrigerate 2 hours or until well chilled.

2. Bring water, butter and rice mix to a boil in medium saucepan. Continue boiling over medium heat 10 minutes or until rice is tender, stirring occasionally. Let cool.

3. Preheat oven to 350°F. Remove waxed paper from ground beef mixture. Spread spinach over ground beef mixture, leaving 1-inch border. Spread cooled rice evenly over spinach. Starting at long end, roll up jelly-roll style, using foil as a guide and removing foil after rolling. Seal edges tightly. Place roulade seam side down in foil-lined 13×9-inch baking pan. Bake, uncovered, about 1 hour. Let stand 15 minutes before serving. Cut into 1-inch slices.

Makes about 8 servings

Fuss-Free Grilling

Honey-Mustard Chicken with Apples

    4 boneless skinless chicken breast (about 4 ounces each)
    **4 sheets (18×12 inches) heavy-duty foil, lightly sprayed with
        nonstick cooking spray**
    Salt and black pepper
    1 medium green apple, cored and cut into eighths
    ¾ cup peach jam
    1 small red bell pepper, diced
    2 tablespoons honey mustard
    1 tablespoon cornstarch
    1 clove garlic, minced
    ½ teaspoon ground ginger
    ¼ cup sliced green onions, for garnish

1. Prepare grill for direct cooking.

2. Place one chicken breast half in center of each sheet of foil. Season with salt and pepper. Place apple wedges beside chicken pieces. Repeat with remaining chicken, foil, salt, pepper and apple.

3. Combine jam, bell pepper, mustard, cornstarch, garlic and ginger in small bowl. Spoon over each chicken breast and apple wedges.

4. Double-fold sides and ends of foil to seal packets, leaving head space for heat circulation. Place on baking sheet.

5. Slide packets off baking sheet onto grill grid. Grill, covered, over medium-high coals 11 to 13 minutes until chicken is no longer pink in center. Carefully open one end of each packet to allow steam to escape. Open packets and transfer mixture to serving plates. Sprinkle with green onions before serving.   *Makes 4 servings*

Honey-Mustard Chicken with Apples

Sweet & Zesty Fish with Fruit Salsa

¼ cup *French's®* Bold n' Spicy Brown Mustard
¼ cup honey
2 cups chopped assorted fresh fruit (pineapple, kiwi,
    strawberries and mango)
1 pound sea bass or cod fillets or other firm-fleshed white fish

1. Preheat broiler or grill. Combine mustard and honey. Stir
2 tablespoons mustard mixture into fruit; set aside.

2. Brush remaining mustard mixture on both sides of fillets. Place in
foil-lined broiler pan. Broil (or grill) fish 6 inches from heat for
8 minutes or until fish is opaque.

3. Serve fruit salsa with fish.   *Makes 4 servings*

Tip: To prepare this meal even faster, purchase cut-up fresh fruit from
the salad bar.

Prep Time: 15 minutes
Cook Time: 8 minutes

Sweet & Zesty Fish With Fruit Salsa

Trout Stuffed with Fresh Mint and Oranges

2 pan-dressed* trout (1 to 1¼ pounds each)
½ teaspoon coarse salt, such as Kosher salt
1 orange, sliced
1 cup fresh mint leaves
1 sweet onion, sliced

*A pan-dressed trout has been gutted and scaled with head and tail removed.

1. Rinse trout under cold running water; pat dry with paper towels.

2. Sprinkle cavities of trout with salt; fill each with orange slices and mint. Cover each fish with onion slices.

3. Spray 2 large sheets of foil with nonstick cooking spray. Place 1 fish on each sheet and seal using Drugstore Wrap technique.**

4. Place foil packets, seam side down, directly on medium-hot coals; grill on covered grill 20 to 25 minutes or until trout flakes easily when tested with fork, turning once.

5. Carefully open foil packets, avoiding hot steam; remove and discard orange-mint stuffing and trout skin. Serve immediately.

Makes 6 servings

**Place the food in the center of an oblong piece of heavy-duty foil, leaving at least a two-inch border around the food. Bring the two long sides together above the food; fold down in a series of locked folds, allowing for heat circulation and expansion. Fold the short ends up and over again. Press folds firmly to seal the foil packet.

"Grilled" Tuna with Vegetables in Herb Butter

4 pieces heavy-duty aluminum foil, each 12×18 inches
1 (7-ounce) pouch of STARKIST® Premium Albacore or Chunk
   Light Tuna
1 cup slivered red or green bell pepper
1 cup slivered yellow squash or zucchini
1 cup pea pods, cut crosswise into halves
1 cup slivered carrots
4 green onions, cut into 2-inch slices
   Salt and black pepper to taste (optional)
Herb Butter
3 tablespoons butter or margarine, melted
1 tablespoon lemon or lime juice
1 clove garlic, minced
2 teaspoons dried tarragon leaves, crushed
1 teaspoon dried dill weed

On each piece of foil, mound tuna, bell pepper, squash, pea pods, carrots and onions. Sprinkle with salt and black pepper.

For Herb Butter, in small bowl stir together butter, lemon juice, garlic, tarragon and dill. Drizzle over tuna and vegetables. Fold edges of each foil square together to make packets.

To grill
Place foil packets about 4 inches above hot coals. Grill for 10 to 12 minutes or until heated through, turning packets over halfway through grill time.

To bake
Place foil packets on baking sheet. Bake in preheated 450°F oven for 15 to 20 minutes or until heated through.

To serve
Cut an "X" on top of each packet; peel back foil.

Makes 4 servings

Cajun Pork Chops with Pineapple

4 boneless pork loin chops, cut ½ inch thick (about
    1 pound total)
2 teaspoons Cajun seasoning
4 sheets (18×12 inches) heavy-duty foil, lightly sprayed with
    nonstick cooking
1 can (15¼ ounces) pineapple tidbits, drained
2 tablespoons frozen orange juice concentrate, thawed
1 tablespoon finely chopped jalapeño pepper*
2 teaspoons Dijon-style mustard
    Chopped fresh parsley (optional)

Jalapeño peppers can sting and irritate the skin; wear rubber gloves when handling peppers and do not touch eyes. Wash hands after handling peppers.

1. Prepare grill for direct cooking.

2. Rub pork chops on both sides with Cajun seasoning. Place one pork chop in center of each sheet of foil.

3. Top pork chops with pineapple. Stir together orange juice concentrate, jalapeño pepper and mustard in small bowl. Spoon sauce over pineapple.

4. Double-fold sides and ends of foil to seal packets, leaving head space for heat circulation. Place on baking sheet.

5. Slide packets off baking sheet onto grill grid. Grill, covered, over medium-high coals 10 to 12 minutes or until no longer pink in center. Carefully open one end of each packet to allow steam to escape. Open packets and transfer to serving plates. Sprinkle with parsley, if desired.

Makes 4 servings

Shanghai Fish Packets

4 orange roughy or tilefish fillets (4 to 6 ounces each)
¼ cup mirin* or Rhine wine
3 tablespoons soy sauce
1 tablespoon dark sesame oil
1½ teaspoons grated fresh ginger
¼ teaspoon red pepper flakes
1 tablespoon peanut or vegetable oil
1 clove garlic, minced
1 package (10 ounces) fresh spinach leaves, stems removed

*Mirin is a sweet Japanese wine available in Japanese markets and the gourmet section of large supermarkets.

1. Prepare grill for direct cooking.

2. Place orange roughy in single layer in large shallow dish. Combine mirin, soy sauce, sesame oil, ginger and red pepper flakes in small bowl; pour over orange roughy. Cover; marinate in refrigerator 20 minutes.

3. Heat peanut oil in large skillet over medium heat. Add garlic; cook and stir 1 minute. Add spinach; cook and stir until wilted, about 3 minutes, tossing with 2 wooden spoons.

4. Place spinach mixture in center of four 12-inch squares of heavy-duty foil. Remove orange roughy from marinade; reserve marinade. Place 1 orange roughy fillet over each mound of spinach. Drizzle reserved marinade evenly over orange roughy. Wrap in foil.

5. Place packets on grid. Grill packets, on covered grill, over medium coals 15 to 18 minutes or until orange roughy flakes easily when tested with fork. *Makes 4 servings*

Shanghai Fish Packet

Sweet & Sour Chicken

2 boneless skinless chicken breasts
2 sheets (18×12 inches) heavy-duty foil, lightly sprayed with
   nonstick cooking spray
   Salt and black pepper
½ medium green bell pepper, cut in short, thin strips
½ medium red bell pepper, cut in short, thin strips
¼ onion, cut in thin wedges
½ cup drained canned pineapple chunks
½ cup orange marmalade
1 tablespoon white vinegar
2 teaspoons cornstarch
2 teaspoons soy sauce
   Hot cooked rice (optional)

1. Prepare grill for direct cooking or preheat oven to 450°F.

2. Place one chicken breast in center of one sheet of foil. Season to taste with salt and pepper.

3. Place half of bell peppers and onion on each chicken breast. Top with half of pineapple chunks.

4. Combine marmalade, vinegar, cornstarch and soy sauce in small bowl; stir until cornstarch is dissolved. Pour half over vegetables.

5. Double fold sides and ends of foil to seal packets, leaving head space for heat circulation. Repeat with remaining chicken, vegetables, pineapple and sauce mixture. Place packets on baking sheet.

6. Slide packets off baking sheet onto grid of covered grill. Grill 12 to 14 minutes over medium-high coals until chicken is no longer pink in center. Or, bake packets on baking sheet 16 to 18 minutes. Carefully open one end of each packet to allow steam to escape. Open packets and transfer mixture to serving plates. Serve with rice, if desired.

Makes 2 servings

Cajun Catfish with Red Beans and Rice

Red Beans and Rice (recipe follows), optional
6 skinless catfish fillets (6 ounces each)
12 frozen deveined shelled large shrimp, thawed
⅓ cup olive oil
1 teaspoon dried thyme leaves
1 teaspoon dried oregano leaves
2 cloves garlic, minced
½ teaspoon black pepper
½ teaspoon salt
⅛ to ¼ teaspoon ground red pepper
6 sheets (15×12 inches) heavy-duty foil, lightly sprayed with nonstick cooking spray

1. Preheat oven to 450°F. Prepare Rice and Beans, if desired.

2. Place catfish and shrimp in resealable plastic food storage bag. Combine oil, thyme, oregano garlic, black pepper, salt and red pepper in small bowl. Add to bag. Seal bag; turn bag to coat fish and shrimp. Marinate 30 minutes.

3. Remove fish and shrimp from marinade; discard remaining marinade. Place one fish fillet in center of 1 foil sheet. Top with 2 shrimp.

4. Double fold sides and ends of foil to seal packet, leaving head space for heat circulation. Repeat with remaining fish, shrimp and foil sheets to make 5 more packets. Place packets on baking sheet.

5. Bake 25 minutes. Let stand 5 minutes. Open packet and transfer contents to serving plates. Serve with Red Beans and Rice.

Makes 6 servings

Red Beans and Rice

½ cup uncooked rice
1 cup water
½ teaspoon salt
1 can (15 ounces) kidney beans, rinsed and drained
1 can (14½ ounces) diced tomatoes, undrained
2 tablespoons bacon bits
1 tablespoon chili powder
1 large heavy-duty foil baking bag (17×15 inches), lightly sprayed with nonstick cooking spray

continued on page 112

Cajun Catfish with Red Beans and Rice

Cajun Catfish with Red Beans and Rice, continued

1. Preheat oven to 450°F.

2. Place rice, water and salt in 2-quart microwavable container; microwave at HIGH 7 minutes.

3. Add remaining ingredients; stir until blended. Place foil bag in 1-inch deep jelly-roll pan; spoon rice mixture into bag. Double fold bag to seal. Shake baking pan to distribute contents of bag evenly.

4. Bake 45 minutes. Let stand 5 minutes. Carefully cut bag open. Fold back top to allow steam to escape; serve.   *Makes 6 (1-cup) servings*

Note: For a milder flavor, reduce chili powder to 2 teaspoons.

Vegetable-Topped Fish Pouches

  4 firm fish fillets, such as flounder, cod or halibut (about
     1 pound)
  1 carrot, cut into very thin strips
  1 rib celery, cut into very thin strips
  1 medium red onion, cut into thin wedges
  1 medium zucchini or yellow squash, sliced
  8 mushrooms, sliced
  ½ cup (about 2 ounces) shredded Swiss cheese
  ½ cup WISH-BONE® Italian Dressing*

Also terrific with Wish-Bone® Robusto Italian or Just 2 Good! Italian Dressing.

On four 18×9-inch pieces heavy-duty aluminum foil, divide fish equally. Evenly top with vegetables, then cheese. Drizzle with Italian dressing. Wrap foil loosely around fillets and vegetables, sealing edges airtight with double fold. Let stand to marinate 15 minutes. Grill or broil pouches, seam sides up, 15 minutes or until fish flakes easily with fork.   *Makes 4 servings*

Easy Pepper Steak and Rice

1 cup uncooked instant rice
4 sheets (18×12 inches) heavy-duty foil, lightly sprayed with
**   nonstick cooking spray**
1 pound boneless beef top sirloin steak, cut into thin strips
¼ cup teriyaki sauce
1 tablespoon plus 1 teaspoon ketchup
1 clove garlic, minced
½ cup canned beef broth
8 ice cubes
1 cup chopped onion
1 large green or red bell pepper, cut in short strips

1. Prepare grill for direct cooking or preheat oven to 450°F.

2. Place ¼ cup rice in center of one sheet of foil. Place beef strips in medium bowl. Combine teriyaki sauce, ketchup and garlic in small bowl; mix well. Pour over beef and mix until beef is coated with sauce.

3. Divide beef into four portions. Arrange four beef strips on foil to enclose rice. Pour 2 tablespoons broth over rice. Top with two ice cubes.

4. Arrange remainder of one portion of beef on ice cubes and rice. Top with a quarter of onion and bell pepper.

5. Double fold sides and ends of foil to seal packet, leaving head space for heat circulation. Repeat with remaining rice, beef, broth, ice cubes and vegetables to make three more packets. Place packets on baking sheet.

6. Slide packets off baking sheet onto grid of covered grill. Grill 12 to 13 minutes over medium-high coals. Or, bake on baking sheet 14 to 15 minutes. Remove from oven. Let stand 5 minutes. Open packets and transfer contents to serving plates.   *Makes 4 servings*

Spaghetti Squash with Black Beans and Zucchini

1 spaghetti squash (about 2 pounds)
2 zucchini, cut lengthwise into ¼-inch-thick slices
  Nonstick cooking spray
2 cups chopped seeded tomatoes
1 can (about 15 ounces) black beans, rinsed and drained
2 tablespoons chopped fresh basil
2 tablespoons olive oil
2 tablespoons red wine vinegar
1 large clove garlic, minced
½ teaspoon salt

1. Pierce spaghetti squash in several places with fork. Wrap in large piece of heavy-duty foil, using Drugstore Wrap technique.* Grill squash on covered grill over medium coals 45 minutes to 1 hour or until easily depressed with back of long-handled spoon, turning a quarter turn every 15 minutes. Remove squash from grill and let stand in foil 10 to 15 minutes.

2. To grill zucchini, spray both sides of zucchini slices with cooking spray. Grill on uncovered grill over medium coals 4 minutes or until tender, turning once.

3. Remove spaghetti squash from foil and cut in half; scoop out seeds. With two forks, comb strands of pulp from each half and place in large salad bowl. Add tomatoes, beans, zucchini and basil. Combine olive oil, vinegar, garlic and salt in small bowl; mix thoroughly. Add to vegetables and toss gently to combine. Serve with grilled French bread and garnish, if desired. *Makes 4 servings*

Place food in the center of an oblong piece of heavy-duty foil, leaving at least a two-inch border around the food. Bring the two long sides together above the food; fold down in a series of locked folds, allowing for heat circulation and expansion. Fold short ends up and over again. Press folds firmly to seal the foil packet.

Spaghetti Squash with Black Beans and Zucchini

Greek-Style Grilled Feta

1 package (8 ounces) feta cheese, sliced in half horizontally
24 (¼-inch) slices small onion
½ green bell pepper, thinly sliced
½ red bell pepper, thinly sliced
½ teaspoon dried oregano leaves
¼ teaspoon garlic pepper or black pepper
24 (½-inch) slices French bread

1. Spray 14-inch-long sheet of foil with nonstick cooking spray. Cut feta into 24 slices. Place onion slices in center of foil and top with feta slices. Sprinkle with bell pepper slices, oregano and garlic pepper.

2. Seal foil using Drugstore Wrap technique.* Place foil packet on grid upside down and grill on covered grill over hot coals 15 minutes. Turn packet over; grill on covered grill 15 minutes more.

3. Open packet carefully and serve immediately on slices of French bread. *Makes 8 servings*

Place the food in the center of an oblong piece of heavy-duty foil, leaving at least a two-inch border around the food. Bring the two long sides together above the food; fold down in a series of locked folds, allowing for heat circulation and expansion. Fold the short ends up and over again. Press folds firmly to seal the foil packet.

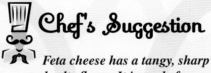 Chef's Suggestion

Feta cheese has a tangy, sharp and salty flavor. It is made from goat's milk. It is very common in Greek cooking and is used for snacking and topping salads.

Vegetable Melange Couscous

¾ cups mesquite chips
4 small new potatoes, cut into eighths
½ pound fresh green beans, trimmed and halved
2 carrots, peeled and diagonally cut into 1-inch pieces
2 plum tomatoes, chopped
1 clove garlic, minced
4 tablespoons dry white wine or water, divided
¼ teaspoon salt, divided
1 can (15 ounces) pinto beans, drained and rinsed
1 package (10 ounces) couscous
½ teaspoon ground cumin
½ teaspoon ground cinnamon
¼ teaspoon red pepper flakes
1 can (14½ ounces) vegetable broth, heated
¼ cup chopped fresh cilantro
　　Lemon peel strips for garnish

1. Cover mesquite chips with water and soak for 20 minutes.

2. Combine vegetables and garlic in large bowl. Divide between 2 sheets of heavy-duty foil. Sprinkle each with 2 tablespoons wine and ⅛ teaspoon salt; seal using Drugstore Wrap technique.*

3. Drain mesquite; sprinkle over coals. Grill packets on covered grill over medium coals 20 to 25 minutes or until vegetables are tender, turning once. Meanwhile, combine beans and 3 tablespoons water in saucepan. Bring to a boil and boil 2 to 3 minutes, stirring occasionally; remove from heat. Remove packets from grill to cool.

4. Combine couscous, cumin, cinnamon and red pepper in 8-inch square baking dish and add hot vegetable broth; cover immediately with foil. Allow to stand 5 minutes; fluff with fork and arrange on platter. Top with vegetables and beans; sprinkle with cilantro. Garnish with strips of lemon peel, if desired. *Makes 4 servings*

Place food in the center of an oblong piece of heavy-duty foil, leaving at least a two-inch border around the food. Bring the two long sides together above the food; fold down in a series of locked folds, allowing for heat circulation and expansion. Fold short ends up and over again. Press folds firmly to seal the foil packet.

Chicken Parcels On The Grill

3 tablespoons MRS. DASH® Tomato Basil Garlic seasoning
⅓ cup extra-virgin olive oil
1 tablespoon lemon juice
½ teaspoon black pepper
4 boneless skinless chicken breast halves cut into 1-inch pieces
2 medium zucchini, cut into ½-inch slices
1 medium red bell pepper, seeded and cut into 1-inch pieces
1 medium red onion, finely chopped
4 tablespoons grated Parmesan cheese
    Aluminum foil

Preheat grill to low. In a large bowl, mix Mrs. Dash Tomato Basil Garlic seasoning, olive oil, lemon juice and black pepper. Add chicken pieces and stir well. Add zucchini, peppers and onion to chicken and mix well. Tear 4 sheets of foil, each approximately 14×12 inches. Divide chicken and vegetable mixture into 4 equal parts. Place each portion in the middle of each piece of foil and wrap tightly. Take 4 more sheets of foil, enough to wrap each package again. Place on grill for 25 minutes. Then, with a sharp knife, cut a large slash across the long end of each package. Open slightly to expose the chicken and vegetables and sprinkle 1 tablespoon of Parmesan cheese over the mixture. Cook for another 5 minutes. Serve in the foil package.   *Makes 4 servings*

Prep Time: 10 minutes
Cook Time: 35 minutes

Grilled Fish, Vegetable & Rice Packets

1 box UNCLE BEN'S® Long Grain & Wild Rice Original Recipe
4 orange roughy or tilapia fish fillets (4 ounces each)
3 tablespoons olive oil
3 tablespoons balsamic vinegar or fresh lemon juice
1 medium red bell pepper, cut into thin 2-inch strips
1 cup thinly sliced zucchini
½ cup thinly sliced red onion
8 button mushrooms, quartered

1. Prepare rice according to package directions. Divide cooked rice evenly between four 15×12-inch pieces of heavy-duty foil; spread out rice slightly in center of foil. Place 1 fish fillet over each portion of rice; season fish with salt and pepper, if desired.

2. In medium bowl, gradually whisk oil into vinegar until combined. Add vegetables; toss gently until coated. Divide vegetables evenly over fish and rice; drizzle any remaining oil mixture over fish.

3. Seal foil packets by bringing the two long sides together above food and folding down in several tight folds, then tightly fold in the short ends.

4. Place foil packets, seam side up, on grid over medium coals. Grill, covered, 15 to 20 minutes or until fish flakes easily when tested with fork. *Makes 4 servings*

Chef's Suggestion

Packets can also be placed on a baking sheet and baked in a preheated 400°F oven for 20 to 25 minutes or until the fish flakes easily when tested with fork.

Greek-Style Loin Roast

    1 boneless pork loin roast (3 pounds)
    ¼ cup olive oil
    ¼ cup lemon juice
    1 teaspoon dried oregano leaves, crushed
    1 teaspoon salt
    1 teaspoon black pepper
    6 cloves garlic, minced
        Spicy Yogurt Sauce (recipe follows)

Place pork loin in large resealable plastic food storage bag. Combine all
remaining ingredients except Spicy Yogurt Sauce in small bowl; pour
over pork. Seal bag and marinate in refrigerator overnight, turning bag
occasionally. Meanwhile, prepare Spicy Yogurt Sauce.

Prepare grill with rectangular foil drip pan. Bank briquets on either side
of drip pan for indirect cooking. Remove pork, discarding marinade.
Place pork on grill over drip pan. Grill, on covered grill, over low coals
1½ hours or to an internal temperature of 155°F. Let rest 10 minutes.
(Internal temperature will rise slightly upon standing.) To serve, thinly
slice roast and serve with Spicy Yogurt Sauce.   *Makes 8 servings*

Spicy Yogurt Sauce: Combine 1 cup plain yogurt, 1 peeled and chopped
cucumber, ¼ cup minced red onion, ½ teaspoon crushed garlic,
½ teaspoon crushed coriander seeds and ¼ teaspoon crushed red pepper
in small bowl; blend well. Cover and refrigerate until ready to serve.

Favorite recipe from *National Pork Board*

Greek-Style Loin Roast

Grilled Paella

1½ to 2 pounds chicken wings or thighs
2 tablespoons plus ¼ cup extra-virgin olive oil, divided
   Salt and black pepper
1 pound garlicky sausage links, such as linguisa, chorizo or
   Italian
1 large onion, chopped
2 large red bell peppers, seeded and cut into thin strips
4 cloves garlic, minced
1 can (14 ounces) diced tomatoes, undrained
4 cups uncooked rice
16 tightly closed live mussels or clams,* scrubbed
½ pound large shrimp,* peeled and deveined with tails intact
1½ cups frozen peas
1 can (about 14 ounces) chicken broth
2 lemons, cut into wedges
1 oval disposable foil pan (about 17×13×3 inches)

Seafood can be omitted; add an additional 1¼ to 1½ pounds chicken.

Brush chicken with 2 tablespoons oil; season with salt and black
pepper. Grill chicken and sausage on covered grill over medium
KINGSFORD® Briquets 15 to 20 minutes or until chicken juices run
clear and sausage is no longer pink in center, turning every 5 minutes.
Cut sausage into 2-inch pieces.

Heat remaining ¼ cup oil in large skillet over medium-high heat. Add
onion, bell peppers and garlic; cook and stir 5 minutes or until
vegetables are tender. Add tomatoes, 1½ teaspoons salt and ½ teaspoon
black pepper; cook about 8 minutes until thick, stirring frequently.
Combine onion mixture and rice in foil pan; spread evenly. Arrange
chicken, sausage, seafood and peas over rice. Bring broth and 6 cups
water to a boil in 3 quart saucepan. Place foil pan on grid over medium
KINGSFORD® briquets; immediately pour boiling broth mixture over
rice. Grill on covered grill about 20 minutes until liquid is absorbed. *Do
not stir.* Cover with foil; let stand 10 minutes. Garnish with lemon
wedges.   *Makes 8 to 10 servings*

Grilled Paella

Bodacious Grilled Ribs

4 **pounds pork loin back ribs**
2 **tablespoons paprika**
2 **teaspoons dried basil leaves**
½ **teaspoon onion powder**
¼ **teaspoon garlic powder**
¼ **teaspoon ground red pepper**
¼ **teaspoon black pepper**
2 **sheets (24×18 inches) heavy-duty foil, lightly sprayed with nonstick cooking spray**
8 **ice cubes**
1 **cup barbecue sauce**
½ **cup apricot all-fruit spread**

1. Prepare grill for direct cooking. Cut ribs into 4- to 6-rib pieces.

2. Combine paprika, basil, onion powder, garlic powder, red pepper and black pepper in small bowl. Rub on both sides of rib pieces. Place 2 pounds of ribs, in single layer, in center of each foil sheet. Place 4 ice cubes on top of each.

3. Double fold sides and ends of foil to seal packets, leaving head space for heat circulation. Place on baking sheet. Stir together barbecue sauce and jam; set aside.

4. Slide packets off baking sheet onto grill grid. Grill, covered, over medium coals 45 to 60 minutes or until tender. Carefully open one end of each packet to allow steam to escape.

5. Open packets and transfer ribs to grill rack. Brush with barbecue sauce mixture. Continue grilling 5 to 10 minutes, brushing with sauce and turning often. *Makes 4 servings*

Super Sandwiches

Hot Antipasto Subs

⅓ cup *French's®* Bold n' Spicy Brown Mustard
3 tablespoons mayonnaise
½ teaspoon dried oregano leaves
4 (6-inch) crusty Italian-style rolls, sliced lengthwise in half
1 jar (6 ounces) marinated artichoke hearts, drained and chopped
¼ cup chopped pitted cured olives
¼ cup sliced roasted red peppers, drained
¾ pound sliced deli meats and cheese such as salami, spiced ham and provolone cheese
1 cup arugula or spinach leaves, washed

1. Preheat oven to 400°F. Combine mustard, mayonnaise and oregano. Spread evenly on both sides of rolls.

2. Layer remaining ingredients on bottom of rolls, dividing evenly. Cover with top half, pressing firmly.

3. Wrap sandwiches in foil. Bake 10 minutes or until hot and cheese melts slightly. *Makes 4 servings*

Prep Time: 20 minutes
Cook Time: 10 minutes

Hot Antipasto Sub

Football Salami Kick-Off

1 large loaf Italian bread*
   HEBREW NATIONAL® Deli Mustard
1 tablespoon vegetable oil
⅔ cup chopped onion
⅓ cup chopped seeded red bell pepper
⅓ cup chopped seeded green bell pepper
1 (12-ounce) HEBREW NATIONAL® Beef Salami or Lean Beef
   Salami Chub, diced
8 eggs, beaten *or* 1½ cups cholesterol-free egg substitute
   Salt
   Freshly ground black pepper

Or, substitute 6 hoagie rolls for Italian bread loaf. Prepare and fill as directed for Italian bread loaf. Wrap each filled hoagie individually in aluminum foil; bake about 15 minutes or until heated through.

Preheat oven to 350°F. Slice bread in half lengthwise. Remove soft bread center; reserve for another use. Spread mustard evenly inside bread shells.

Heat oil in large nonstick skillet over medium heat. Add onion; cook 4 minutes. Add bell peppers; cook 4 minutes or until peppers are tender, stirring occasionally. Add salami; cook until heated through. Add eggs; increase heat to medium-high. Cook, stirring until eggs are set. Season with salt and pepper to taste.

Fill bread shells with salami mixture. Close sandwich; wrap tightly in aluminum foil. Bake 20 minutes or until heated through. Cut sandwich crosswise into 6 slices.   *Makes 6 servings*

Bean and Vegetable Burritos

1 tablespoon olive oil
1 medium onion, thinly sliced
1 jalapeño pepper,* seeded and minced
1 tablespoon chili powder
3 cloves garlic, minced
2 teaspoons dried oregano leaves
1 teaspoon ground cumin
1 large sweet potato, baked, cooled, peeled and diced *or* 1 can
   (16 ounces) yams in syrup, rinsed, drained and diced
1 can (about 15 ounces) black beans or pinto beans, rinsed and
   drained
1 cup frozen corn, thawed, drained
1 green bell pepper, chopped
2 tablespoons lime juice
¾ cup (3 ounces) shredded reduced-fat Monterey Jack cheese
4 flour tortillas (10 inches)
  Sour cream (optional)

Jalapeño peppers can sting and irritate the skin. Wear rubber gloves when handling peppers and do not touch eyes. Wash hands after handling peppers.

Preheat oven to 350°F. Heat oil in large saucepan or Dutch oven over medium-high heat. Add onion and cook, stirring often, 10 minutes or until golden. Add jalapeño pepper, chili powder, garlic, oregano and cumin; stir 1 minute more. Add 1 tablespoon water and stir; remove from heat. Stir in sweet potato, beans, corn, bell pepper and lime juice.

Spoon 2 tablespoons cheese in center of each tortilla. Top with 1 cup filling. Fold all 4 sides around filling to enclose. Place burritos seam side down on baking sheet. Cover with foil and bake 30 minutes or until heated through. Serve with sour cream, if desired.

Makes 4 servings

Bean and Vegetable Burrito

Melted SPAM® & Cheese Poppy Seed Sandwiches

½ cup butter or margarine, softened
3 tablespoons prepared mustard
1 tablespoon poppy seeds
8 slices cracked wheat bread
1 (12-ounce) can SPAM® Classic, cut into 8 slices
4 (1-ounce) slices American cheese

Heat oven to 375°F. In small bowl, combine butter, mustard and poppy seeds. Spread butter mixture on bread slices. Place 2 slices of SPAM® on each of 4 bread slices. Top SPAM® with 1 slice of cheese. Top with remaining 4 bread slices. Wrap sandwiches in foil. Bake 10 to 15 minutes or until cheese is melted. *Makes 4 servings*

Chef's Suggestion

*These sandwiches are delicious
for lunch, dinner or even a snack.
They are also very easy to prepare.*

Open-Faced Oven Reubens

2 slices rye bread

2 sheets (18×12 inches) heavy-duty foil, lightly sprayed with
   nonstick cooking spray

1½ cups fresh sauerkraut, divided

2 fully cooked, smoked Polish sausages, split open

2 sandwich-style dill pickle slices

2 slices Swiss cheese

¼ cup Thousand Island salad dressing, divided

1. Preheat toaster oven or oven to 450°F.

2. Place one bread slice on each sheet of foil. Top with sauerkraut, sausage, pickle and cheese.

3. Double fold sides and ends of foil to seal packets, leaving head space for heat circulation. Place packets on toaster oven tray or baking sheet.

4. Bake 30 to 35 minutes or until sandwiches are hot.

5. Carefully open one end of packet to allow steam to escape. Open packets and transfer contents top serving plates. Serve with dressing.

Makes 2 servings

 **Chef's Suggestion**

Make Thousand Island salad dressing by mixing together ¼ cup reduced-fat mayonnaise, 2 tablespoons ketchup and 1 tablespoon chopped dill pickle. Add pickle juice or lemon juice to taste.

Spicy Meatball Sandwiches

1 large (17×15 inches) foil cooking bag
1 jar (26 ounces) marinara sauce
1 pound frozen pre-cooked Italian-style meatballs
½ cup chopped green bell pepper
⅓ cup sliced ripe olives
2 teaspoons dried Italian seasoning
¼ teaspoon ground red pepper
6 slices mozzarella cheese, halved lengthwise
6 hoagie buns
3 tablespoons finely shredded Parmesan cheese

1. Prepare grill for direct cooking.

2. Place bag in 1-inch deep baking pan. Combine marinara sauce, meatballs, bell pepper, olives, Italian seasoning and red pepper in large bowl. Spoon into bag, arranging in even layer. Double fold open side of bag, leaving head space for heat circulation.

3. Slide bag off pan onto grill grid. Grill, covered, over medium-high coals 11 to 13 minutes or until meatballs are hot. Carefully open bag to allow steam to escape.

4. Meanwhile, place two pieces cheese on bottom of each bun. Spoon meatball mixture into buns. Sprinkle with Parmesan cheese.

Makes 6 servings

Spicy Meatball Sandwich

New Orleans Heros with Olive Pesto

½ cup oil-cured olives, pitted
½ cup pimento stuffed olives, rinsed and drained
½ cup slivered almonds
2 cloves garlic, chopped
⅓ cup *French's*® Bold n' Spicy Brown Mustard
2 tablespoons olive oil
6 mini baguette rolls, split
1 pound sliced luncheon meats and cheese, such as smoked
    ham, salami and provolone cheese

Place olives, almonds and garlic in food processor. Cover and process until finely chopped. Add mustard and oil. Cover and process until well blended. Spread olive pesto on rolls, dividing evenly. Arrange luncheon meats and cheese over pesto. Cover with top halves of rolls.

Wrap heros in heavy-duty foil. Place heros on grid. Cook over medium-high coals 10 minutes or until rolls are crispy. Serve warm.

Makes 6 servings

Prep Time: 20 minutes
Cook Time: 10 minutes

New Orleans Hero with Olive Pesto

Tandoori Chicken Breast Sandwiches with Yogurt Sauce

4 boneless skinless chicken breasts (about 12 ounces)
1 tablespoon lemon juice
¼ cup plain nonfat yogurt
2 large cloves garlic, minced
1½ teaspoons finely chopped fresh ginger
¼ teaspoon ground cardamom
¼ teaspoon ground red pepper
   Yogurt Sauce (recipe follows)
2 rounds whole wheat pita bread
½ cup grated carrot
½ cup finely shredded red cabbage
½ cup finely chopped red bell pepper

1. Lightly score chicken breasts 3 or 4 times with sharp knife. Place in medium bowl; sprinkle with lemon juice and toss to coat.

2. Combine yogurt, garlic, ginger, cardamom and ground red pepper in small bowl; add to chicken. Coat all pieces well with marinade; cover and refrigerate at least 1 hour or overnight.

3. Remove chicken from refrigerator 15 minutes before cooking. Preheat broiler. Prepare Yogurt Sauce; set aside.

4. Line broiler pan with foil. Arrange chicken on foil (do not let pieces touch) and brush with any remaining marinade. Broil 3 inches from heat about 5 to 6 minutes per side or until chicken is no longer pink in center.

5. Cut pitas in half crosswise; gently open. Place one chicken breast in each pita half with 2 tablespoons each of carrot, cabbage and bell pepper. Drizzle sandwiches with Yogurt Sauce. Garnish, if desired.

Makes 4 servings

Yogurt Sauce

½ cup plain nonfat yogurt
2 teaspoons minced red onion
1 teaspoon minced cilantro
¼ teaspoon ground cumin
¼ teaspoon salt
   Dash ground red pepper

Blend all ingredients well in small bowl. Cover and refrigerate until ready to use.

Makes about ½ cup

Tandoori Chicken Breast Sandwich with Yogurt Sauce

Italian Celebration Sandwich

¼ cup extra-virgin olive oil
2 cloves garlic, mashed
1 white onion, thinly sliced
1 green bell pepper, seeded and cut into strips
1 red bell pepper, seeded and cut into strips
  Salt
  Ground black pepper
1 package (1 pound) PERDUE® Fresh Seasoned Lean Turkey
    Sausage, Hot or Sweet Italian
6 hoagy or submarine rolls, split
1 cup prepared marinara sauce
1 cup shredded mozzarella cheese

Prepare grill for cooking. In small bowl, combine oil and garlic. In medium bowl, combine onions and bell peppers; add half of oil mixture and toss to coat thoroughly. Add salt and pepper to taste. Fold heavy-duty aluminum foil to form 2 or 3 packets; poke holes in foil with fork.

Grill sausages, uncovered, 5 to 6 inches over medium-hot coals 15 minutes until cooked through, turning often. Add vegetables to foil packets and grill alongside sausages until tender. Brush rolls with remaining garlic oil; grill about 5 minutes until lightly toasted. Meanwhile, warm sauce in small pan at edge of grill. To serve, place a sausage on bottom half of each roll; top with sauce, cheese, vegetables and top of roll.   *Makes 6 servings*

Asian-Seasoned Barbecue Pork Sandwiches

1 large (17×15 inches) foil cooking bag
1½ pounds lean pork stew meat, cut into 1½-inch pieces
¾ cup barbecue sauce
¼ cup teriyaki marinade
2 tablespoons honey
2 tablespoons all-purpose flour
½ teaspoon hot pepper sauce
6 hamburger buns

1. Prepare grill for direct cooking.

2. Place bag in 1-inch deep jelly-roll pan. Toss together meat, barbecue sauce, marinade, honey, flour and hot pepper sauce in large bowl. Spoon into bag, arranging in even layer. Double-fold open side of bag, leaving head space for heat circulation.

3. Slide bag from pan onto grill grid. Grill, covered, over medium coals 15 to 20 minutes or until meat is tender. Carefully open bag. Transfer mixture to bowl. Using two forks, coarsely shred pork. Stir pork together with sauce. Serve on buns. *Makes 6 servings*

SPAM™ Hot Vegetable Salad Sandwiches

6 unsliced whole wheat buns or Kaiser rolls
1 (7-ounce) can SPAM® Classic, cubed
1 cup (4 ounces) shredded Monterey Jack cheese
1 tomato, chopped
½ cup finely chopped broccoli
½ cup thinly sliced carrots
¼ cup chopped onion
2 tablespoons peppercorn ranch-style salad dressing

Heat oven to 350°F. Cut thin slice from top of each bun; reserve. Remove soft center from each bun, leaving ½-inch shell. Combine remaining ingredients. Spoon into buns, pressing filling into buns. Top with reserved bun tops. Wrap each sandwich tightly in aluminum foil. Bake 20 minutes or until thoroughly heated and cheese is melted.

Makes 6 servings

Chicken and Mozzarella Melts

2 cloves garlic, crushed
4 boneless skinless chicken breasts (about ¾ pound)
  Nonstick cooking spray
⅛ teaspoon salt
⅛ teaspoon black pepper
1 tablespoon prepared pesto sauce
4 small hard rolls, split
12 fresh spinach leaves
8 fresh basil leaves* (optional)
3 plum tomatoes, sliced
½ cup (2 ounces) shredded part-skim mozzarella cheese

*Omit basil leaves if fresh are unavailable. Do not substitute dried basil leaves.

1. Preheat oven to 350°F. Rub garlic on all surfaces of chicken. Spray medium nonstick skillet with cooking spray; heat over medium heat until hot. Add chicken; cook 5 to 6 minutes on each side or until no longer pink in center. Sprinkle with salt and pepper.

2. Brush pesto sauce onto bottom halves of rolls; layer with spinach, basil, if desired, and tomatoes. Place chicken in rolls; sprinkle cheese evenly over chicken. (If desired, sandwiches may be prepared up to this point and wrapped in aluminum foil. Refrigerate until ready to bake. Bake in preheated 350°F oven until chicken is warm, about 20 minutes.)

3. Wrap sandwiches in aluminum foil; bake about 10 minutes or until cheese is melted.   *Makes 4 servings*

Chicken and Mozzarella Melt

Simple Sides

Broccoli in Cheese Sauce

1 bag (16 ounces) frozen broccoli florets
1 sheet (24×12 inches) heavy-duty foil, lightly sprayed with
    nonstick cooking spray
1 can (10¾ ounces) condensed Cheddar cheese soup, undiluted
1 medium red or yellow bell pepper, cut into 1-inch pieces
¼ cup chopped onion
¼ cup milk
1½ teaspoons Worcestershire sauce
⅛ teaspoon black pepper

1. Preheat oven to 450°F. Place frozen broccoli in center of sheet of foil. Fold foil up around broccoli to create pan.

2. Combine soup, bell pepper, onion, milk, Worcestershire sauce and black pepper in medium bowl; stir to blend. Pour over broccoli.

3. Double fold sides and ends of foil to seal packet, leaving head space for heat circulation. Place packet on baking sheet.

4. Bake 25 minutes or until vegetables are tender. Remove from oven. Carefully open one end of packet to allow steam to escape. Open packet and transfer broccoli mixture to serving bowl.   *Makes 6 servings*

Broccoli in Cheese Sauce

Low-Fat Cajun Wedges

4 russet potatoes
  Nonstick cooking spray
1 tablespoons cajun seasoning or other seasoning, such as paprika
  Purple kale and fresh sage leaves, for garnish

1. Preheat oven to 400°F. To prepare potatoes, scrub under running water with soft vegetable brush; rinse. Dry well. (Do not peel.) Line baking sheet with aluminum foil and spray with cooking spray.

2. Cut potatoes in half lengthwise; then cut each half lengthwise into 3 wedges. Place potatoes, skin side down, in single layer on prepared baking sheet.

3. Spray potatoes lightly with cooking spray and sprinkle with seasoning.

4. Bake 25 minutes or until browned and fork-tender. Garnish, if desired. Serve immediately.   *Makes 4 servings*

Low-Fat Potato Chips: Follow step 1 as directed. Slice potatoes crosswise as thin as possible with chef's knife or mandoline slicer. Place in single layer on prepared baking sheet; spray and season as directed. Bake 10 to 15 minutes or until browned and crisp. Serve immediately.

Low-Fat Cottage Fries: Follow step 1 as directed. Cut potatoes crosswise into ¼-inch-thick slices. Place in single layer on prepared baking sheet; spray and season as directed. Bake 15 to 20 minutes or until browned and fork-tender. Serve immediately.

Low-Fat Cajun Wedges

Mashed Sweet Potatoes with Roasted Red Onions

6 cloves garlic, peeled
1 red onion, quartered, then sliced into 1-inch slices
¼ cup olive oil
   Salt and freshly ground black pepper
2 pounds sweet potatoes, cooked and mashed (about 2½ to
      3 cups)
1 tablespoon butter

1. Preheat oven to 300°F. Place the garlic and onion on an 11×8-inch sheet of foil, drizzle with the oil and sprinkle with salt and pepper. Fold foil edges over vegetables to make a closed packet. Place packet in a glass baking dish. Bake about 1 hour or until onions are soft and translucent.

2. In a medium bowl, combine the mashed potatoes and butter with the roasted garlic, onion and any juices. Serve immediately.

Makes 6 servings

Grilled Summer Vegetables Alouette®

1 large aluminum foil cooking bag
3 cups fresh broccoli florets
3 cups sliced summer squash (any type)
2 medium red bell peppers, cut in strips
1 cup sliced mushrooms
1 (6.5-ounce) package or two (4-ounce) packages ALOUETTE®
   Garlic & Herbs

Preheat grill to medium high. Open foil bag, layer vegetables evenly inside, and spoon Alouette cheese on top. Seal bag by double-folding end. Place on grill and cook 8 to 10 minutes. Using oven mitts, carefully place bag on baking sheet and cut open, allowing steam to escape. If bag sticks to grill rack, cut open and remove vegetables (after grill cools, peel off bag).

Makes 6 servings

For oven cooking: Preheat oven to 450°F. Insert ingredients as above. Bake sealed bag on baking sheet 20 to 25 minutes.

Bubble & Squeak Casserole

½ cup condensed Cheddar cheese soup, undiluted
¼ milk or chicken broth
2 medium red potatoes, cut into thin slices
2 sheets (18×12 inches) heavy-duty foil, lightly sprayed with
    nonstick cooking spray
1 small onion, cut into thin slices
2 cups shredded cabbage
¼ teaspoon salt
⅛ teaspoon black pepper

1. Preheat toaster oven or oven to 450°F.

2. Mix together soup and milk in small bowl until smooth. Set aside.

3. Place half of potato slices on each sheet of foil, overlapping slices. Top with onion and cabbage. Sprinkle with salt and pepper. Top with soup mixture.

4. Double fold sides and ends of foil to seal packets, leaving head space for heat circulation. Place packets onto toaster oven tray or baking sheet.

5. Bake 30 to 35 minutes or until vegetables are tender.

6. Carefully open one end of each packets to allow steam to escape. Open packets and transfer contents to serving plates.

Makes 2 servings

Serving suggestion: If desired, top each serving of Bubble & Squeak Casserole with a fried egg or cooked sausage patty.

Chutney'd Squash Circles

2 acorn squash (1 pound each)
2 tablespoons butter or margarine
½ cup prepared chutney
2 tablespoons water
  Purple kale and scented geranium leaves for garnish*

*Use only non-toxic leaves.

1. Preheat oven to 400°F. Slice tip and stem end from squash. Scoop out and discard seeds. Cut squash crosswise into ¾-inch rings.

2. Tear off 18-inch square of heavy-duty foil. Center foil in 13×9-inch baking dish. Dot foil with butter and place squash on butter, slightly overlapping rings. Spoon chutney over slices and sprinkle with water.

3. Bring foil on long sides of pan together in center, folding over to make tight seam. Fold ends to form tight seal.

4. Bake 20 to 30 minutes until squash is fork-tender. Transfer to warm serving plate. Pour pan drippings over squash. Garnish with kale, if desired.

Makes 4 side-dish servings

Chef's Suggestion

Acorn squash has an acorn shape and weighs from one to three pounds. The skin is dark green with patches of orange and the flesh is a deep orange. It has a sweet flavor.

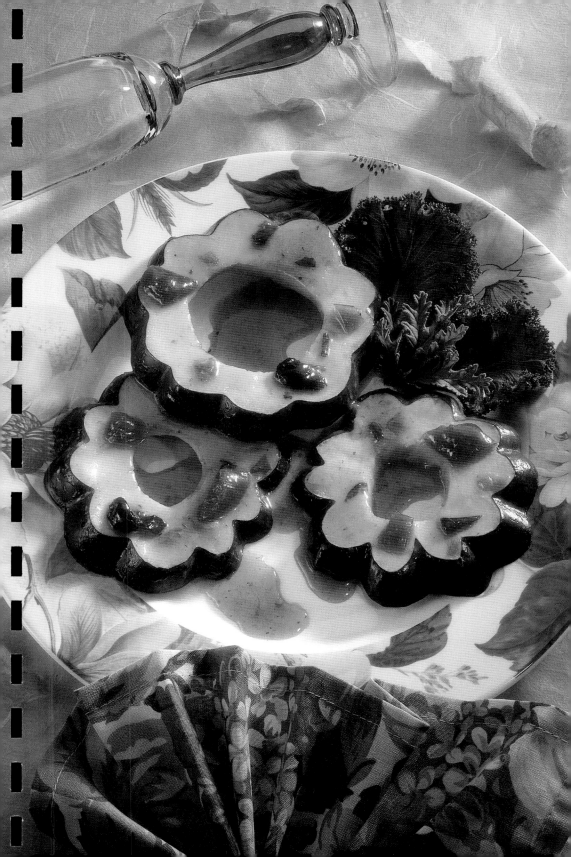

Grilled Potato Salad

1 envelope LIPTON® RECIPE SECRETS® Onion Soup Mix*
⅓ cup BERTOLLI® Olive Oil
2 tablespoons red wine vinegar
1 clove garlic, finely chopped
**2 pounds small red or all-purpose potatoes, cut into 1-inch
     cubes**
**1 tablespoon chopped fresh basil, chopped *or* 1 teaspoon dried
     basil leaves, crushed**
Freshly ground black pepper

**Also terrific with LIPTON® RECIPE SECRETS® Onion Mushroom or Golden Onion
Soup Mix.*

1. In large bowl, blend soup mix, oil, vinegar and garlic; stir in potatoes.

2. Grease 30×18-inch sheet of heavy-duty aluminum foil; top with
potato mixture. Wrap foil loosely around mixture, sealing edges airtight
with double fold. Place on another sheet of 30×18-inch foil; seal edges
airtight with double fold in opposite direction.

3. Grill, shaking package occasionally and turning package once,
40 minutes or until potatoes are tender. Spoon into serving bowl and
toss with basil and pepper. Serve slightly warm or at room temperature.

Makes 4 servings

Oven Method: Preheat oven to 450°F. Prepare foil packet as above.
Place in large baking pan on bottom rack and bake, turning packet once,
40 minutes or until potatoes are tender. Toss and serve as above.

Grilled Potato Salad

Lemon 'n' Dill Barbecued Corn-on-the-Cob

6 medium (8 to 12 ounces each) unhusked whole ears corn
3 tablespoons soft (50% reduced-calorie) margarine
   Grated peel of ½ SUNKIST® lemon
1 tablespoon fresh squeezed juice from 1 SUNKIST® lemon
1 tablespoon chopped fresh dill or 1 teaspoon dry dill weed
   Salt and white pepper to taste

Carefully pull back husks (do not detach) and remove silk from each ear of corn. Rinse well in cold water. In small bowl, beat margarine, lemon peel and lemon juice until well blended. Stir in dill. To prepare each ear of corn, place on 12- to 16-inch-long piece of foil; brush corn with ⅙ of margarine mixture. Sprinkle lightly with salt and pepper. Replace husks around corn; individually wrap each securely in foil. Grill 6 inches above glowing coals or on MEDIUM heat of gas barbecue 25 to 35 minutes, turning every 5 minutes. To serve, remove foil and cut off husks.   *Makes 6 servings*

Cheddary Pull Apart Bread

1 round loaf corn or sour dough bread (1 pound)*
½ cup (1 stick) butter or margarine, melted
¼ cup French's® Classic Yellow® Mustard
½ teaspoon chili powder
½ teaspoon seasoned salt
¼ teaspoon garlic powder
1 cup (4 ounces) shredded Cheddar cheese

*You can substitute one 12-inch loaf Italian bread for the corn bread.

Cut bread into 1-inch slices, cutting about ⅔ of the way down through loaf. (Do not cut through bottom crust.) Turn bread ¼ turn and cut across slices in similar fashion. Combine butter, mustard and seasonings in small bowl until blended. Brush cut surfaces of bread with butter mixture. Spread bread "sticks" apart and sprinkle cheese inside. Wrap loaf in foil.

Place packet on grid. Cook over medium coals about 30 minutes or until bread is toasted and cheese melts. Pull bread "sticks" apart to serve.   *Makes about 8 servings*

Prep Time: 15 minutes
Cook Time: 30 minutes

Garden Fresh Vegetable Bundles

6 large sheets of heavy aluminum foil
PAM® No-Stick Cooking Spray
2 cups cubed potatoes (1-inch squares)
2 cups sliced zucchini (2-inch slices)
1 cup sliced carrots (¼-inch slices)
1 cup diced red bell pepper (1-inch dice)
1 cup diced green bell pepper (1-inch dice)
1 cup broccoli florets (1-inch pieces)
1 cup diced sweet onion (1-inch dice)
1 large ear of corn, cut into 6 pieces
¼ cup WESSON® Vegetable Oil
3 teaspoons Creole seasoning
Garlic salt

Preheat oven to 450°F. Spray *each* sheet of foil with PAM® Cooking Spray. In a large bowl, combine *next* 8 ingredients, ending with corn. Toss with Wesson® Oil. Evenly divide vegetable mixture among prepared sheets of foil. Sprinkle ½ teaspoon Creole seasoning on *each* vegetable packet. Sprinkle with desired amount of garlic salt. Bring sides of foil to center and fold over to seal. Fold ends to center, creating a tight bundle. Repeat with *remaining* packets. Place bundles on cookie sheet; bake for 30 minutes or until vegetables are tender.

Makes 6 servings

Chef's Suggestion

This recipe also works great on the grill!

Zucchini-Tomato Bake

1 pound eggplant, coarsely chopped
2 cups zucchini slices
2 cups mushroom slices
3 sheets (18×12 inches) heavy-duty foil, lightly sprayed with
    nonstick cooking spray
2 teaspoons olive oil
½ cup chopped onion
½ cup chopped fresh fennel (optional)
2 cloves garlic, minced
1 can (14½ ounces) no-salt-added whole tomatoes, undrained
1 tablespoon no-salt-added tomato paste
2 teaspoons dried basil leaves
1 teaspoon sugar

1. Preheat oven to 400°F. Divide eggplant, zucchini and mushrooms into 3 portions. Arrange each portion on foil sheet.

2. Heat oil in small skillet over medium heat. Add onion, fennel, if desired, and garlic. Cook and stir 3 to 4 minutes or until onion is tender. Add tomatoes with juice, tomato paste, basil and sugar. Cook and stir about 4 minutes or until sauce thickens.

3. Pour sauce over eggplant mixture. Double-fold sides and ends of foil to seal packets, leaving head space for heat circulation. Place on baking sheet.

4. Bake 30 minutes. Remove from oven. Carefully open one end of each packet to allow steam to escape. Open and transfer contents to serving dish. Garnish, if desired. *Makes 6 servings*

Oven Roasted Potatoes and Onions with Herbs

3 pounds unpeeled red potatoes, cut into 1½-inch cubes
1 large sweet onion, such as Vidalia or Walla Walla, coarsely chopped
3 tablespoons olive oil
2 tablespoons butter, melted, or bacon drippings
3 cloves garlic, minced
¾ teaspoon salt
¾ teaspoon black pepper
⅓ cup packed chopped mixed fresh herbs, such as basil, chives, parsley, oregano, rosemary, sage, tarragon and thyme

1. Preheat oven to 450°F. Arrange potatoes and onion in large shallow roasting pan lined with foil.

2. Combine oil, butter, garlic, salt and pepper in small bowl. Drizzle over potatoes and onion; toss well to combine.

3. Bake 30 minutes. Stir and bake 10 minutes more. Add herbs; toss well. Continue baking 10 to 15 minutes or until vegetables are tender and browned. Transfer to serving bowl. Garnish with fresh rosemary, if desired. *Makes 6 servings*

Chef's Suggestion

Vidalia, Maui and Walla Walla are all very sweet onions. They have taken their names from the areas where they grow: Vidalia, Georgia; Maui, Hawaii; and Walla Walla, Washington. Vidalia are generally the sweetest.

Stuffed Portabellos with Sausage

4 portabello mushroom caps, wiped clean with damp cloth
Cooking spray
6 ounces reduced-fat bulk sausage
1 cup chopped yellow onion
1 medium red bell pepper, chopped
1 medium zucchini, chopped
1 teaspoon dried thyme
2 slices whole wheat bread, grated in blender or hand grater,
(about 1 cup)
⅓ cup water
½ cup chopped parsley leaves
Salt to taste

1. Preheat oven 350°F. Remove stem from each mushroom cap. Chop stems and set aside.

2. Coat both sides of each mushroom cap with cooking spray. Place on baking sheet and set aside.

3. Place a 12-inch nonstick skillet over medium-high heat until hot. Coat skillet with cooking spray. Add sausage and cook until browned, breaking up large pieces while cooking, stirring constantly. Drain cooked sausage on paper towels.

4. To pan residue, add onion, zucchini, mushroom stems and thyme. Cook 4 minutes or until onion is translucent, stirring frequently.

5. Remove skillet from heat. Stir in sausage, bread crumbs, water, parsley and salt to taste. Top each mushroom with ¾ cup filling and cover with foil. Bake 30 minutes or until tender.

6. Remove from oven and let stand 5 minutes to absorb flavors. (Don't skip this step, the flavors mellow and blend with mushrooms.)

Makes 4 servings

Potatoes Au Gratin

2 medium unpeeled baking potatoes (about 1 pound)
2 sheets (18×18 inches) heavy-duty foil, generously sprayed
with nonstick cooking spray
1 cup (4 ounces) shredded Cheddar cheese
½ cup (2 ounces) shredded Swiss cheese
1 tablespoon butter or margarine
1 tablespoon plus 1½ teaspoons all-purpose flour
1 cup milk
1 tablespoon Dijon mustard
⅛ teaspoon salt
⅛ teaspoon black pepper

1. Preheat oven to 400°F.

2. Cut potatoes into thin slices. Arrange quarter of potato slices on each sheet of foil. Top with half the cheeses. Repeat layers using remaining potatoes and cheeses. Fold foil up around potatoes.

3. Melt butter in medium saucepan over medium heat. Stir in flour; cook 1 minute. Stir in milk, mustard, salt and pepper; bring to a boil. Reduce heat and cook, stirring constantly, until mixture thickens. Carefully pour milk mixture into packets.

4. Double fold sides and ends of foil to seal packets. Place packets on baking sheet.

5. Bake 25 minutes. Remove packets from oven. Carefully open tops of packets. Return to oven and bake 10 minutes more until potatoes are tender and tops are brown. Remove from oven and let stand 10 minutes before serving. *Makes 2 servings*

Stuffed Bell Peppers

 1 cup chopped fresh tomatoes
 1 teaspoon chopped fresh cilantro
 1 jalapeño pepper,* seeded and chopped (optional)
 ½ clove garlic, finely minced
 ½ teaspoon dried oregano leaves, divided
 ¼ teaspoon ground cumin
 6 ounces lean ground round
 ½ cup cooked brown rice
 ¼ cup cholesterol-free egg substitute *or* 2 egg whites
 2 tablespoons finely chopped onion
 ¼ teaspoon salt
 ⅛ teaspoon black pepper
 2 large bell peppers, any color, seeded and cut in half
    lengthwise

Jalapeño peppers can sting and irritate the skin; wear rubber gloves when handling peppers and do not touch eyes. Wash hands after handling peppers.

1. Preheat oven to 400°F.

2. Combine tomatoes, cilantro, jalapeño pepper, if desired, garlic, ¼ teaspoon oregano and cumin in small bowl. Set aside.

3. Thoroughly combine beef, rice, egg substitute, onion, salt and black pepper in large bowl. Stir in ⅔ cup of tomato mixture. Spoon filling evenly into pepper halves.

4. Spray 4 (12×12-inch) sheets heavy-duty foil with nonstick cooking spray. Place each pepper half on foil sheet. Double fold sides and ends of foil to seal packets. Place packets on baking sheet.

5. Bake 45 minutes or until meat is browned and vegetables are tender. Remove from oven. Carefully open one end of each packet to allow steam to escape. Open packets and transfer pepper halves to serving plates. Serve with remaining tomato mixture.   *Makes 4 servings*

Stuffed Bell Peppers

Green Beans with Savory Mushroom Sauce

2 packages (10 ounces each) frozen French-style green beans, thawed
1 can (10¾ ounces) condensed cream of mushroom soup, undiluted
2 tablespoons dry vermouth or dry white wine
1½ cups mushrooms, sliced
½ teaspoon salt
½ teaspoon dried thyme leaves
¼ teaspoon black pepper
2 sheets (18×12 inches) heavy-duty foil, lightly sprayed with nonstick cooking spray
1 cup crushed prepared croutons or canned fried onion rings

1. Preheat oven to 450°F. Combine all ingredients except foil and croutons in large bowl. Mix until well blended.

2. Divide mixture between foil sheets. Double fold sides and ends of foil to seal packets, leaving head space for heat circulation. Place packets on baking sheet.

3. Bake 20 minutes or until hot. Remove from oven. Carefully open one end of each packet to allow steam to escape. Open packets and transfer contents to serving bowl. Sprinkle with croutons.

Makes 6 to 8 servings

Green Beans with Savory Mushroom Sauce

Summer Squash Gratin

8 ounces refrigerated grated potatoes
1 cup yellow squash, thinly sliced
1 cup zucchini, thinly sliced
1 cup frozen pepper stir-fry blend, thawed
½ teaspoon dried oregano leaves
¼ teaspoon salt
½ teaspoon ground black pepper
½ cup grated Parmesan cheese or shredded sharp Cheddar
   cheese
4 sheets (12×12 inches each) heavy-duty foil, lightly sprayed
   with nonstick cooking spray
1 tablespoon butter or margarine, cut into 8 pieces

1. Preheat oven to 375°F.

2. Layer ¼ of *each* potatoes, yellow squash, zucchini, stir-fry blend, oregano, salt, black pepper and cheese on foil sheet. Top with 2 pieces of butter. Double fold sides and ends of foil to seal packet. Repeat with remaining potatoes, vegetables, seasonings, cheese and butter to make 4 packets. Place packets on baking sheet.

3. Bake 15 to 20 minutes or until vegetables are just tender. Remove from oven. Carefully open one end of packets to allow steam to escape. Open tops of packets and return to oven. Bake 10 minutes longer or until cheese is lightly browned. *Makes 4 servings*

Chili Roasted Turkey with Cool Cucumber-Mango Salsa

2 (16-ounce) packages PERDUE® Fit 'N Easy® Skinless &
   Boneless Turkey Breast Tenderloins
1 (1.25-ounce) package taco seasoning
1 teaspoon ground cumin
Salsa
2 ripe mangos, diced
1 cucumber, peeled, seeded and diced
¼ cup red onion, minced
¼ cup lime juice
1 tablespoon vegetable oil
   Salt and pepper, to taste
   Lime slices to garnish, optional

Preheat oven to 500°F. Set turkey tenderloins on a foil-lined sheet pan. In a small bowl, stir together taco seasoning and cumin. Rub all sides of turkey with spice mix. Roast turkey 18 to 20 minutes, turning once, until firm. Remove and set aside.

While turkey is roasting, make salsa. Stir together mango, cucumber, red onion, lime juice and oil. Season to taste with salt and pepper.

To serve, slice turkey. Divide turkey among 6 plates and top with salsa. Garnish with lime slices, if desired.   *Makes 6 servings*

Prep Time: 20 minutes
Cook Time: 18 to 20 minutes

Grilled Sweet Potato Packets with Pecan Butter

**4 sweet potatoes (about 8 ounces each), peeled and cut into
¼-inch-thick slices**
**1 large sweet or Spanish onion, thinly sliced and separated into
rings**
3 tablespoons vegetable oil
⅓ cup butter or margarine, softened
2 tablespoons packed light brown sugar
¼ teaspoon salt
¼ teaspoon ground cinnamon
¼ cup chopped pecans, toasted

1. Prepare barbecue grill for direct cooking.

2. Alternately place potato slices and onion rings on four 14×12-inch
sheets of heavy-duty foil. Brush tops and sides with oil to prevent
drying.

3. Double fold sides and ends of foil to seal packets. Place foil packets
on grid. Grill packets, on covered grill, over medium coals 25 to
30 minutes or until potatoes are fork-tender.

4. Meanwhile, to prepare Pecan Butter, combine butter, sugar, salt and
cinnamon in small bowl; mix well. Stir in pecans. Carefully open
packets; top each with dollop of Pecan Butter.   *Makes 4 servings*

Chef's Suggestion

*Sweet potatoes should be heavy
for their size, firm, smooth and
free of bruises or blemishes.
Check for decay, which often
begins at the tips. Choose potatoes
of similar size and shape if they
are to be cooked whole.*

Grilled Sweet Potato Packets with Pecan Butter

Potatoes au Gratin

4 to 6 medium unpeeled baking potatoes (about 2 pounds)
2 cups (8 ounces) shredded Cheddar cheese
1 cup (4 ounces) shredded Swiss cheese
2 tablespoons butter or margarine
3 tablespoons all-purpose flour
2½ cups milk
2 tablespoons Dijon mustard
¼ teaspoon salt
¼ teaspoon black pepper

1. Preheat oven to 400°F. Grease 13×9-inch baking dish.

2. Cut potatoes into thin slices. Layer potatoes in prepared dish. Top with cheeses.

3. Melt butter in medium saucepan over medium heat. Stir in flour; cook 1 minute. Stir in milk, mustard, salt and pepper; bring to a boil. Reduce heat and cook, stirring constantly, until mixture thickens. Pour milk mixture over cheese. Cover pan with foil.

4. Bake 30 minutes. Remove foil and bake 15 to 20 minutes more until potatoes are tender and top is brown. Remove from oven and let stand 10 minutes before serving.   *Makes 6 to 8 servings*

Chef's Suggestion

At home, store potatoes in a cool, dark, dry, well-ventilated place. Do not refrigerate potatoes. It is important to protect potatoes from light; that may cause them to turn green and lose quality.

Potatoes au Gratin

Grilled Banana Squash with Rum & Brown Sugar

2 pounds banana squash or butternut squash
2 tablespoons dark rum or apple juice
2 tablespoons melted butter
2 tablespoons brown sugar

Cut squash into 4 pieces; discard seeds. Place squash in microwavable baking dish. Cover with vented plastic wrap. Microwave at HIGH 5 to 7 minutes, turning once. Discard plastic wrap; pierce flesh of squash with fork at 1-inch intervals. Place squash in foil pan. Combine rum and butter; brush over squash. Sprinkle with sugar. Grill squash on covered grill over medium KINGSFORD® Briquets 20 to 30 minutes until squash is tender. *Makes 4 servings*

Honey-Mustard Roasted Potatoes

4 large baking potatoes (about 2 pounds)
½ cup Dijon mustard
¼ cup honey
½ teaspoon crushed dried thyme leaves
Salt and pepper to taste

Peel potatoes and cut each into 6 to 8 pieces. Cover potatoes with salted water in large saucepan. Bring to a boil over medium-high heat. Cook potatoes 12 to 15 minutes or until just tender. Drain. Combine mustard, honey and thyme in small bowl. Toss potatoes with honey-thyme mustard in large bowl until evenly coated. Arrange potatoes on foil-lined baking sheet coated with nonstick cooking spray. Bake at 375°F 20 minutes or until potatoes begin to brown around edges. Season to taste with salt and pepper. *Makes 4 servings*

Favorite recipe from *National Honey Board*

Glazed Maple Acorn Squash

1 large acorn or golden acorn squash
1 sheet (24×18 inches) heavy-duty foil, lightly sprayed with nonstick cooking spray
¼ cup water
2 tablespoons pure maple syrup
1 tablespoon margarine or butter, melted
¼ teaspoon ground cinnamon

1. Preheat oven to 375°F.

2. Cut ends from squash. Cut squash crosswise into four equal slices. Discard seeds and membrane. Place squash on foil sheet. Fold sides of foil up around squash. Add water.

3. Double fold sides and ends of foil to seal packet, leaving head space for heat circulation. Place packet on baking sheet. Bake 30 minutes or until tender. Remove packet from oven.

4. Combine syrup, margarine and cinnamon in small bowl; mix well. Carefully open one end of packet to allow steam to escape and pour off water. Open top of packet. Brush squash with syrup mixture, letting excess pool in center of squash. Do not reseal packet.

5. Return packet to oven; bake 10 minutes or until syrup mixture is bubbly. Transfer contents of packet to serving dish.

Makes 4 servings

Herbed Mushroom Vegetable Medley

4 ounces button or crimini mushrooms
1 medium red or yellow bell pepper, cut into ¼-inch-wide strips
1 medium zucchini, cut crosswise into ¼-inch-thick slices
1 medium yellow squash, cut crosswise into ¼-inch-thick slices
3 tablespoons butter or margarine, melted
1 tablespoon chopped fresh thyme leaves *or* 1 teaspoon dried
    thyme leaves
1 tablespoon chopped fresh basil leaves *or* 1 teaspoon dried
    basil leaves
1 tablespoon chopped fresh chives or green onion tops
1 clove garlic, minced
¼ teaspoon salt
¼ teaspoon black pepper

1. Prepare barbecue grill for direct cooking.

2. Cut thin slice from base of mushroom stems with paring knife; discard. Thinly slice mushroom stems and caps. Combine mushrooms, bell pepper, zucchini and squash in large bowl. Combine butter, thyme, basil, chives, garlic, salt and black pepper in small bowl. Pour over vegetable mixture; toss to coat well.

3. Transfer mixture to 20×14-inch sheet of heavy-duty foil; wrap. Place foil packet on grid. Grill packet, on covered grill, over medium coals 20 to 25 minutes or until vegetables are fork-tender. Open packet carefully to serve.   *Makes 4 to 6 servings*

Herbed Mushroom Vegetable Medley

Neptune's Spaghetti Squash

1 spaghetti squash (about 3 pounds)
4 tablespoons olive oil
1 clove garlic, minced
½ pound medium shrimp, peeled and deveined
½ pound bay scallops
½ cup fresh or frozen peas
¼ cup sun-dried tomatoes in oil, drained and chopped*
½ teaspoon dried basil leaves
¼ cup freshly grated Parmesan cheese
    Fresh basil leaves and tarragon flowers for garnish

*Or, substitute 2 plum tomatoes, seeded and chopped, for sun-dried tomatoes. (To seed tomatoes, cut in half. Remove seeds with spoon; discard.)

1. Preheat oven to 375°F. To bake squash, pierce in several places with cooking fork to vent steam.

2. Place squash in large foil-lined baking dish; bake 20 minutes. Turn squash upside down; cook 25 minutes more or until easily depressed with finger.** Cut in half immediately to prevent further cooking.

3. Heat oil over medium-high heat in large skillet. Cook and stir garlic in hot oil just until it begins to brown. Remove garlic; discard. Add shrimp, scallops, peas, tomatoes and basil. Cook and stir 1 to 2 minutes until shrimp turn pink and scallops are opaque. Set aside.

4. Cut squash in half. Scoop out seeds from squash.

5. To remove spaghetti strands from squash, "comb" strands from each half of rind with two forks. Transfer to warm serving platter. Top with cooked seafood mixture; toss gently to coat. Sprinkle with cheese. Garnish, if desired. Serve immediately.   *Makes 6 servings*

**Larger squash may take longer to cook.

Neptune's Spaghetti Squash

Sweet Potato and Apple Casserole

1 sheet (24×18 inches) heavy-duty foil, generously sprayed with
    nonstick cooking spray
½ cup packed dark brown sugar
½ teaspoon ground cinnamon
¼ teaspoon ground mace or nutmeg
2 pounds sweet potatoes, peeled and quartered
  Salt
3 tablespoons butter, divided
2 Granny Smith apples, peeled, quartered and cored
½ cup granola cereal

1. Preheat oven to 375°F. Place foil loosely in 8×8-inch or 9×9-inch baking pan.

2. Mix brown sugar, cinnamon and mace in small bowl. Place ⅓ of potato slices in center of foil sheet. Sprinkle with salt to taste. Crumble half the sugar mixture over potatoes and dot with 1 tablespoon butter.

3. Slice each apple quarter into four wedges. Layer half the apples on top of potatoes. Repeat layers using potatoes, sugar mixture, butter and apples. Top with remaining potatoes and 1 tablespoon butter.

4. Double fold sides and ends of foil to seal packet, leaving head space for heat circulation.

5. Bake in baking pan 25 minutes. Remove from oven. Carefully open one end of packet to allow steam to escape. Open top of packet; spoon liquid in bottom of packet over potatoes. Sprinkle with granola; do not reseal packet. Bake 35 minutes more or until potatoes are fork-tender. Garnish, if desired. *Makes 6 servings*

Pilsner Parmesan Potatoes

4 pounds Yukon Gold potatoes, peeled and sliced thin
1 cup minced Vidalia onion
½ cup heavy cream
12 ounces pilsner beer
1 tablespoon flour
1 cup grated aged Parmesan cheese
1 teaspoon paprika
Salt and pepper to taste

1. Preheat oven to 350°F. Butter a 13×9 baking dish. Place potato slices in the prepared dish. Sprinkle with minced onion.

2. Mix together cream, beer, flour, Parmesan cheese, paprika and salt and pepper to taste. Pour over the potato mixture and stir gently to coat potato slices evenly. Cover baking dish with foil.

3. Bake 30 minutes, covered; remove foil. Bake 15 to 20 minutes more, or until potatoes are golden brown and bubbly. Remove from oven and let sit for 15 minutes before serving.   *Makes 4 to 6 servings*

No-Mess Desserts

Mango-Banana Foster

2 medium mangoes, peeled, seeded and chopped
2 ripe, firm bananas, cut into ¾-inch-thick slices
8 maraschino cherries, halved
4 sheets (18 ×12 inches each) heavy-duty foil
½ cup firmly packed brown sugar
2 tablespoons rum *or* 2 tablespoons orange juice plus
    ¼ teaspoon rum extract
½ teaspoon ground cinnamon
    Vanilla ice cream

1. Prepare grill for direct cooking.

2. Place mango, banana and cherries in center of each piece of foil. Stir together brown sugar, rum and cinnamon in small bowl. Spoon brown sugar mixture over fruit mixture.

3. Double-fold sides and ends of foil to seal packets, leaving head space for heat circulation. Place on baking sheet.

4. Slide packets off baking sheet onto grill grid. Grill, covered, over medium-high coals 3 to 5 minutes or until hot. Carefully open one end of each packet to allow steam to escape.

5. Meanwhile, spoon ice cream into serving bowls. Open packets and pour fruit over of ice cream. *Makes 4 servings*

Mango-Banana Foster

Steamed Southern Sweet Potato Custard

1 can (16 ounces) cut sweet potatoes, drained
1 can (12 ounces) evaporated milk, divided
½ cup packed light brown sugar
2 eggs, lightly beaten
1 teaspoon ground cinnamon
½ teaspoon ground ginger
¼ teaspoon salt
   Whipped cream (optional)
   Ground nutmeg (optional)

Slow Cooker Directions

Process sweet potatoes with about ¼ cup milk in food processor or blender until smooth. Add remaining milk, brown sugar, eggs, cinnamon, ginger and salt; process until well mixed. Pour into ungreased 1-quart soufflé dish. Cover tightly with foil. Crumple large sheet (about 15×12 inches) of foil; place in bottom of slow cooker. Pour 2 cups water over foil. Make foil handles* and place soufflé dish on top of foil strips.

Transfer dish to slow cooker using foil handles; lay foil strips over top of dish. Cover and cook on HIGH 2½ to 3 hours or until skewer inserted in center comes out clean. Using foil strips, lift dish from slow cooker and transfer to wire rack. Uncover; let stand 30 minutes. Garnish with whipped cream and nutmeg, if desired.   *Makes 4 servings*

To make foil handles, tear off three 18×3-inch strips of heavy-duty foil. Crisscross the strips so they resemble the spokes of a wheel. Place the dish or food in the center of the strips. Pull the foil strips up and over and place into the slow cooker. Leave them in while you cook so you can easily lift the item out again when ready.

Steamed Southern Sweet Potato Custard

Individual Chocolate Coconut Cheesecakes

12 foil bake cups
1 cup chocolate cookie crumbs
¼ cup butter or margarine, melted
2 packages (8 ounces each) cream cheese, softened
⅓ cup sugar
2 eggs
1 teaspoon vanilla
¼ teaspoon coconut extract (optional)
½ cup flaked coconut
½ cup semi-sweet chocolate chips
1 teaspoon shortening

1. Preheat oven to 325°F. Line twelve 2½-inch muffin cups with foil bake cups.

2. Combine cookie crumbs and butter in small bowl. Press onto bottoms of bake cups.

3. Combine cream cheese and sugar in large bowl. Beat 2 minutes at medium speed of electric mixer until well blended. Add eggs, vanilla and coconut extract, if desired. Beat just until blended. Stir in coconut.

4. Carefully spoon about ¼ cup cream cheese mixture into each bake cup. Bake 18 to 22 minutes or until nearly set. Cool 30 minutes in pan on wire rack. Remove from pan. Peel away foil bake cups.

5. Combine chocolate chips and shortening in small saucepan. Cook and stir over low heat until chocolate chips are melted. Drizzle over tops of cheesecakes. Let stand 20 minutes. Cover and refrigerate until ready to serve.

Makes 12 servings

Individual Chocolate Coconut Cheesecakes

Vanilla Mousse in Fluted Chocolate Cups

¾ cup (7.25 ounce bottle) SMUCKER'S® Magic Shell Chocolate or
   Chocolate Fudge Ice Cream Topping
1 package (24) foil baking cups (1¾-inch in diameter)
⅔ cup evaporated milk, thoroughly chilled
1 egg
¼ cup sugar
   Salt
1 teaspoon vanilla
24 mint leaves, if desired
24 maraschino cherry slices, if desired

Pour Magic Shell into small bowl. With small, dry pastry brush, thinly and evenly coat insides of baking cups with Magic Shell. Chill in freezer for several minutes. Coat and freeze each cup at least 3 more times. Store cups in freezer.

Whip evaporated milk until stiff. Beat in egg, sugar, a pinch of salt and vanilla. Spoon or pipe mousse into fluted chocolate cups. Freeze until firm. Before serving, carefully remove foil and garnish each cup with 1 mint leaf and 1 maraschino cherry slice. For extended storage, cover tops of cups lightly with plastic wrap and store in freezer up to 1 week.

Makes 24 servings

Backyard S'Mores

2 milk chocolate bars (1.55 ounces each), cut in half
8 large marshmallows
4 whole graham crackers (8 squares)

Place each chocolate bar half and 2 marshmallows between 2 graham cracker squares. Wrap in lightly greased foil. Place on grill over medium-low KINGSFORD® Briquets about 3 to 5 minutes or until chocolate and marshmallows are melted. (Time will vary depending upon how hot coals are and whether grill is open or covered.)

Makes 4 servings

Easy Gingerbread

1 sheet (24×12 inches) heavy-duty foil
1 cup all-purpose flour
⅓ cup packed light brown sugar
1 teaspoon ground ginger
¾ teaspoon ground cinnamon
½ teaspoon baking soda
½ teaspoon baking powder
¼ teaspoon salt
¼ teaspoon ground cloves
1 egg
½ cup milk
⅓ cup melted butter
¼ cup unsulphured molasses
   Powdered sugar (optional)

1. Preheat oven to 350°F. Center foil over 8×5×2½-inch loaf pan. Gently ease foil into pan. You will have a 1-inch overhang of foil on each side and a 5-inch overhang on both ends. Generously spray foil with nonstick cooking spray.

2. Combine flour, brown sugar, ginger, cinnamon, baking soda, baking powder, salt and cloves in medium bowl; mix well.

3. In separate small bowl, beat egg. Stir in milk, butter and molasses until well mixed.

4. Add liquid mixture to dry ingredients; stir until smooth. Pour batter into foil-lined pan. Fold overhanging foil sides and ends over batter to cover batter completely; crimp foil, leaving head space for cake as it rises.

5. Bake 45 minutes or until toothpick inserted in center comes out clean. Remove from oven. Carefully open foil to allow steam to escape. Cool in pan on wire rack 10 to 15 minutes. Place serving plate over pan and invert gingerbread onto plate. Peel off foil.

6. Serve warm, or at room temperature sprinkled with powdered sugar, if desired. *Makes 6 servings*

Peach-Pecan Upside-Down Cake

    1 can (8½ ounces) peach slices
    ⅓ cup packed brown sugar
    2 tablespoons butter or margarine, melted
    ¼ cup chopped pecans
    1 package (16 ounces) pound cake mix, plus ingredients to
        prepare mix
    ½ teaspoon almond extract
        Whipped cream (optional)

Slow Cooker Directions

1. Generously grease 7½-inch slow cooker bread-and-cake bake pan or casserole dish; set aside.

2. Drain peach slices, reserving 1 tablespoon of juice. Combine reserved peach juice, brown sugar and butter in prepared bake pan. Arrange peach slices on top of brown sugar mixture. Sprinkle with pecans.

3. Prepare cake mix according to package directions; stir in almond extract. Spread over peach mixture. Cover pan. Make foil handles as described below for easier removal of pan from slow cooker. Place pan into slow cooker. Cover; cook on HIGH 3 hours.

4. Use foil handles to remove pan from slow cooker. Cool, uncovered, on wire rack for 10 minutes. Run narrow spatula around sides of pan; invert onto serving plate. Serve warm with whipped cream, if desired.

Makes 10 servings

Foil Handles: Tear off three 18×2-inch strips of heavy foil or use regular foil folded to double thickness. Crisscross foil strips in spoke design and place pan on center of strips. Pull foil strips up and over pan.

Prep Time: 10 minutes
Cook Time: 3 hours

Peach-Pecan Upside-Down Cake

Special Treat No-Bake Squares

½ cup plus 1 teaspoon butter, divided
¼ cup granulated sugar
¼ cup unsweetened cocoa powder
1 egg
¼ teaspoon salt
1½ cups graham cracker crumbs
¾ cup flaked coconut
½ cup chopped pecans
⅓ cup butter, softened
1 package (3 ounces) cream cheese, softened
1 teaspoon vanilla
1 cup powdered sugar
1 (2-ounce) dark sweet or bittersweet candy bar, broken into
 ½-inch pieces

Line 9-inch square baking pan with foil, shiny side up, allowing 2-inch overhang on sides. Set aside.

For crust, combine ½ cup butter, granulated sugar, cocoa, egg and salt in medium saucepan. Cook over medium heat, stirring constantly, until mixture thickens, about 2 minutes. Remove from heat; stir in graham cracker crumbs, coconut and pecans. Press evenly into prepared baking pan.

For filling, beat ⅓ cup softened butter, cream cheese and vanilla in small bowl until smooth. Gradually beat in powdered sugar. Spread over crust; refrigerate 30 minutes.

For glaze, combine candy bar pieces and remaining 1 teaspoon butter in small resealable plastic bag; seal. Microwave at HIGH 50 seconds. Turn bag over; heat at HIGH 40 to 50 seconds or until melted. Knead bag until candy bar is smooth. Cut tiny corner off bag; drizzle chocolate over filling. Refrigerate until firm, about 20 minutes. Remove squares from pan using foil. Cut into 1½-inch squares.

Makes about 3 dozen squares

Special Treat No-Bake Squares

Spiced Grilled Bananas

    3 large ripe firm bananas
 ¼ cup golden raisins
    3 tablespoons packed brown sugar
 ½ teaspoon ground cinnamon
 ¼ teaspoon ground nutmeg
 ¼ teaspoon ground cardamom or coriander
    2 tablespoons margarine, cut into 8 pieces
    1 tablespoon fresh lime juice
      Vanilla low-fat frozen yogurt (optional)
      Additional fresh lime juice (optional)

1. Spray grillproof 9-inch pie plate with nonstick cooking spray. Cut bananas diagonally into ½-inch-thick slices. Arrange, overlapping, in prepared pie plate. Sprinkle with raisins.

2. Combine sugar, cinnamon, nutmeg and cardamom in small bowl; sprinkle over bananas and raisins and dot with margarine pieces. Cover pie plate tightly with foil. Place on grid and grill, covered, over low coals 10 to 15 minutes or until bananas are hot and tender.

3. Carefully remove foil and sprinkle with 1 tablespoon lime juice. Serve over low-fat frozen yogurt and sprinkle with additional lime juice, if desired. Garnish as desired. *Makes 4 servings*

Reese's® Peanut Butter and Milk Chocolate Chip Fudge

 1½ cups sugar
 ⅔ cup (5-ounce can) evaporated milk
    2 tablespoons butter
 1½ cups miniature marshmallows
 1¾ cups (11-ounce package) REESE'S® Peanut Butter and Milk
      Chocolate Chips
    1 teaspoon vanilla extract

1. Line 8×8×2-inch baking pan with foil. Butter foil. Set aside.

2. Combine sugar, evaporated milk and butter in heavy medium saucepan. Cook over medium heat, stirring constantly, to a full rolling boil. Boil, stirring constantly, 5 minutes. Remove from heat; stir in marshmallows, chips and vanilla. Stir until marshmallows are melted. Pour into prepared pan. Refrigerate 1 hour or until firm. Cut into squares. Store tightly covered in a cool, dry place.

Makes about 1¾ pounds fudge

Spiced Grilled Bananas

Broiled Pineapple with Spiced Vanilla Sauce

- 3 ounces reduced-fat cream cheese
- ¼ cup granulated sugar
- ¼ cup undiluted evaporated milk or half-and-half
- ¼ teaspoon pumpkin pie spice or Chinese 5-spice powder
- ¼ teaspoon vanilla
- 1 sheet (14×12 inches) heavy-duty foil
- 2 teaspoons butter
- 2 thick, round slices fresh pineapple, skin and eyes trimmed
- 1 tablespoon light brown sugar

1. Preheat broiler. Place cream cheese, granulated sugar, milk, pumpkin pie spice and vanilla in food processor or blender; process until smooth. Refrigerate.

2. Coat center of foil sheet with butter. Place pineapple slices side by side on foil. Sprinkle with brown sugar. Fold up sides and ends of foil form container around pineapple, leaving top of container open. Place container on baking sheet.

3. Broil pineapple 4 inches from heat source 10 to 12 minutes until surface of pineapple is bubbling and flecked with brown. Watch pineapple closely during last 5 minutes of broiling to avoid burning.

5. Remove from oven. Transfer pineapple to serving plates. Serve immediately with cream cheese mixture. *Makes 2 servings*

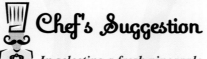 Chef's Suggestion

In selecting a fresh pineapple, look for crown leaves that are dark green and fresh looking. Also, sniff the pineapple—a fragrant pineapple aroma is a good sign of ripeness. And finally, select fruit that is heavy for its size—the larger the fruit, the better the economy and the more there is to enjoy!

Chocolate Bread Pudding

1 sheet (12×12 inches) heavy-duty foil
4 slices firm-textured white bread
1 egg
1 tablespoon unsweetened cocoa powder
¾ cup milk
3 tablespoons sugar
1 teaspoon vanilla
⅛ teaspoon ground cinnamon
⅓ cup semisweet chocolate chips
Whipped topping or sweetened whipped cream (optional)

1. Preheat oven to 350°F. Generously spray center of foil with nonstick cooking spray. Toast bread just enough to dry it, but not enough to brown it. Cool slightly and cut into cubes.

2. Beat egg in large bowl; whisk in cocoa until well blended. Stir in milk, sugar, vanilla and cinnamon. Add bread cubes and chocolate chips; stir until all bread cubes are moistened. Let stand until most of liquid is absorbed.

3. Place a portion of bread cube mixture in center of foil. Carefully shape foil up and around bread cubes to form bowl about 4-inches in diameter. Add remainder of bread cube mixture. Adjust foil, if necessary, leaving foil bowl open at top. Place foil bowl on baking sheet.

4. Bake 35 to 40 minutes or until set. Remove from oven. Cool 15 minutes. Serve warm or at room temperature garnished with whipped topping, if desired. *Makes 4 servings*

Note: If desired, chocolate milk may be substituted for milk and cocoa. Cinnamon bread may be substituted for white bread; omit ground cinnamon.

Chocolate-Almond Meringue Puffs

  2 tablespoons granulated sugar
  3 packages sugar substitute
1½ teaspoons unsweetened cocoa powder
  2 egg whites, room temperature
  ½ teaspoon vanilla
  ¼ teaspoon cream of tartar
  ¼ teaspoon almond extract
  ⅛ teaspoon salt
1½ ounces sliced almonds
  3 tablespoons sugar-free seedless raspberry fruit spread

1. Preheat oven to 275°F. Combine granulated sugar, sugar substitute and cocoa powder in small bowl; set aside.

2. Place egg whites in small bowl; beat at high speed of electric mixer until foamy. Add vanilla, cream of tartar, almond extract and salt; beat until soft peaks form. Add sugar mixture, 1 tablespoon at a time, beating until stiff peaks form.

3. Line baking sheet with foil. Spoon 15 equal mounds of egg white mixture onto foil. Sprinkle mounds with almonds.

4. Bake 1 hour. Turn oven off but do not open oven door. Leave puffs in oven 2 hours longer or until completely dry. Remove from oven; cool completely.

5. Stir fruit spread and spoon about ½ teaspoon onto each meringue just before serving. *Makes 15 servings*

 Chef's Suggestion

Puffs are best if eaten the same day they're made. If necessary, store in airtight container, adding fruit topping at time of serving.

Chocolate-Almond Meringue Puffs

Cinnamon-Raisin-Banana Bread Pudding

1 egg, beaten
2 tablespoons light brown sugar
1 tablespoon half-and-half or undiluted evaporated milk
¼ teaspoon cinnamon
¼ teaspoon vanilla
1 banana
1 tablespoon lemon juice
3 slices cinnamon-raisin bread
1 sheet (18×12 inches) heavy-duty foil, generously sprayed with
    nonstick cooking spray
2 teaspoons butter, softened and divided
2 tablespoons reduced-fat spreadable cream cheese, divided
1 tablespoon raisins
    Vanilla ice cream (optional)

1. Preheat oven or toaster oven to 350°F.

2. Mix together egg, brown sugar, half-and-half, cinnamon and vanilla
in small bowl. Set aside.

3. Peel and chop banana; place in small bowl. Sprinkle with lemon juice
and set aside.

4. Butter one side of one slice of bread with 1 teaspoon butter. Lay
bread, buttered side down, on foil. Spread bread slice with 1 tablespoon
cream cheese. Fold foil edges up to form close-fitting container around
bread.

5. Spoon 2 tablespoons egg mixture onto bread slice. Arrange half the
banana cubes on bread. Sprinkle with half the raisins. Spread remaining
1 tablespoon cream cheese on one side of one piece of bread. Place
bread slice on bananas, cream cheese side down. Spoon 2 tablespoons
egg mixture over bread slice. Top with remaining banana and raisins.
Spread remaining 1 teaspoon butter on one side of remaining bread
slice. Cut bread slice into cubes. Place bread cubes on banana. Drizzle
remaining egg mixture over bread cubes. Do not seal foil container.

6. Place foil container on baking sheet. Bake 30 minutes or until
pudding is set and top is golden brown and crusty. Remove from oven.
Transfer bread pudding to serving plates. Serve with ice cream, if
desired. *Makes 2 to 3 servings*

Mississippi Mud Bars

¾ **cup packed brown sugar**
½ **cup butter, softened**
1 **egg**
1 **teaspoon vanilla**
½ **teaspoon baking soda**
¼ **teaspoon salt**
1 **cup plus 2 tablespoons all-purpose flour**
1 **cup (6 ounces) semisweet chocolate chips, divided**
1 **cup (6 ounces) white chocolate chips, divided**
½ **cup chopped walnuts or pecans**

Preheat oven to 375°F. Line a 9-inch square pan with foil; grease foil.
Beat sugar and butter in large bowl until blended and smooth. Beat in
egg and vanilla until light. Blend in baking soda and salt. Add flour,
mixing until well blended. Stir in ¾ cup each semisweet and white
chocolate chips and nuts. Spread dough in prepared pan. Bake 23 to
25 minutes or until center feels firm. (Do not overbake.) Remove from
oven; sprinkle remaining ¼ cup each semisweet and white chocolate
chips over top. Let stand until chips melt; spread evenly over bars. Cool
in pan on wire rack until chocolate is set. Cut into 2¼×1-inch bars.

Makes about 3 dozen bars

 *Chef's Suggestion*

*When lining the pan with foil,
allow the edges of the foil sheet to
overhang the edges of the pan;
grease the foil. When the bars are
cool, lift them out of the pan using
the foil handles.*

Easy Carrot Cake

1 sheet (24×12 inches) heavy-duty foil
1 cup all-purpose flour
1 teaspoon baking soda
1 teaspoon ground cinnamon
½ teaspoon ground allspice
1 teaspoon salt
¾ cup brown sugar
2 large eggs
¾ cup canola oil
1 teaspoon vanilla
1 package (10 ounces) ready-to-use shredded carrots
½ cup raisins
½ cup chopped walnuts
1 container (16 ounces) cream cheese-flavored frosting
    (optional)

1. Preheat oven 375°F. Center foil over 9×5×3-inch loaf pan. Gently ease foil into pan, leaving a 1-inch overhang on sides of pan and 5-inch overhand on ends. Generously spray foil with nonstick cooking spray. (See Note.)

2. Sift flour, baking soda, cinnamon, allspice and salt into medium bowl. Set aside.

3. Beat brown sugar and eggs in medium bowl with electric mixer at medium speed until light and creamy. Add oil and vanilla; beat until smooth, about 3 minutes. Gradually add flour mixture to sugar mixture, beating well after each addition. Stir in carrots, raisins and walnuts.

4. Pour batter into prepared pan. Fold overhanging foil over batter to cover completely; crimp foil, leaving head space for cake to rise.

5. Bake 1 hour or until toothpick inserted into center comes out clean. Carefully open foil to allow steam to escape. Cool completely in pan on wire rack. Lift cake from pan; unwrap and transfer to plate. Frost top of cake with frosting, if desired. *Makes 8 servings*

Note: Center foil over back of pan and mold to fit smoothly. Then ease shaped foil into pan with long edges hanging over both ends.

Spiced Pear with Vanilla Ice Cream

1 sheet (18×12 inches) heavy-duty foil
2 teaspoons butter, softened
1 tablespoon light brown sugar
¼ teaspoon pumpkin pie spice
1 large Bosc pear, halved lengthwise and cored
    Lemon juice
2 scoops vanilla ice cream

1. Preheat toaster oven or oven to 450°F. Coat center of foil with butter.

2. Combine sugar and pumpkin pie spice in small bowl. Sprinkle sugar mixture over butter. Sprinkle cut sides of pear halves with lemon juice. Place pear halves, cut side down, side by side on sugar mixture.

3. Double fold sides and ends of foil to seal foil packet, leaving head space for heat circulation. Place packet on toaster oven tray or baking sheet.

4. Bake 40 minutes or until pear halves are tender. Remove from oven. Let stand 15 minutes.

5. Open packet and transfer pear halves to serving plates. Spoon sauce over pears. Serve with ice cream. *Makes 2 servings*

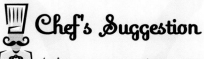 Chef's Suggestion

Anjou pears are autumn pears that are oval in shape. They have a green skin that ripens to a yellow-ish-green color. Anjou pears have a buttery, sweet flavor. They are good for snacking, salads and poaching.

Spiced Pear with Vanilla Ice Cream

Chocolate Frosted Peanut Butter Cupcakes

⅓ cup creamy or chunky reduced-fat peanut butter
⅓ cup butter, softened
½ cup granulated sugar
¼ cup packed brown sugar
2 eggs
1 teaspoon vanilla
1¾ cups all-purpose flour
1½ teaspoons baking powder
¼ teaspoon salt
1¼ cups milk
Peanut Butter Chocolate Frosting (page 208)

1. Preheat oven to 350°F. Line 18 (2½-inch) muffin cups with foil baking cups.

2. Beat peanut butter and butter in large bowl with electric mixer at medium speed until smooth; beat in sugars until well mixed. Beat in eggs and vanilla.

3. Combine flour, baking powder and salt in medium bowl. Add flour mixture to peanut butter mixture alternately with milk, beginning and ending with flour mixture.

4. Pour batter into prepared muffin cups. Bake 23 to 25 minutes or until cupcakes spring back when touched and toothpicks inserted in centers come out clean. Cool in pans on wire racks 10 minutes; remove from pans and cool completely.

5. Prepare Peanut Butter Chocolate Frosting. Frost each cupcake with about 1½ tablespoons frosting. *Makes 1½ dozen cupcakes*

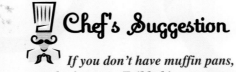 Chef's Suggestion

If you don't have muffin pans, don't worry. Foil baking cups are sturdy enough to be used without muffin pans; simply place the baking cups on a baking sheet and fill.

Chocolate Frosted Peanut Butter Cupcakes

Peanut Butter Chocolate Frosting

4 cups powdered sugar
⅓ cup unsweetened cocoa powder
4 to 5 tablespoons milk, divided
3 tablespoons creamy peanut butter

Combine powdered sugar, cocoa, 4 tablespoons milk and peanut butter in large bowl. Beat with electric mixer at low speed until smooth, scraping bowl frequently. Beat in additional 1 tablespoon milk until desired spreading consistency. *Makes about 2½ cups frosting*

Grilled Peaches with Raspberry Sauce

1 package (10 ounces) frozen raspberries, thawed
1½ teaspoons lemon juice
3 tablespoons brown sugar
1 teaspoon ground cinnamon
1 tablespoon rum (optional)
4 medium peaches, peeled, halved and pitted
2 teaspoons butter
Fresh mint sprigs (optional)

1. Combine raspberries and lemon juice in food processor fitted with metal blade; process until smooth. Chill in refrigerator.

2. Combine brown sugar, cinnamon and rum, if desired, in medium bowl; roll peach halves in mixture. Place peach halves, cut side up, on foil. Dot with butter. Fold foil over peaches, leaving head space for steam; seal foil. Grill over medium coals for 15 minutes.

3. To serve, spoon 2 tablespoons raspberry sauce over each peach half. Garnish with fresh mint sprig, if desired. *Makes 4 servings*

Grilled Peaches with Raspberry Sauce

Baked Cinnamon Apples

4 large Granny Smith or Rome Beauty apples
4 sheets (18×12 inches) heavy-duty foil, lightly sprayed with
   nonstick cooking spray
⅓ cup brown sugar, packed
¼ cup dried cranberries
½ teaspoon ground cinnamon
2 tablespoons butter, cut into 4 pieces
   Vanilla ice cream

1. Preheat oven to 450°F. Core apples. Using paring knife, trim off
½-inch strip around top of each apple. Place each apple in center of foil
sheet.

2. Mix brown sugar, cranberries and cinnamon in small bowl. Fill
apples with sugar mixture, sprinkling any excess around pared rim.
Place 1 piece butter on sugar mixture; press gently.

3. Double fold sides and ends of foil to seal packets, leaving head space
for heat circulation. Place packets on baking sheet.

4. Bake 20 minutes. Remove from oven. Carefully open foil packets;
shape foil around apples. Bake 10 minutes more or until apples are
tender. Remove from oven. Transfer apples to bowls; spoon remaining
liquid over apples. Serve warm apples with ice cream.

Makes 6 servings

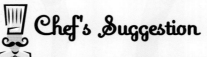 Chef's Suggestion

*Crisp, tart, juicy Granny Smith
apples are not only delicious eaten
raw, but are also excellent for
baking because they keep their
texture. And unlike other apples,
you can enjoy these green-skinned
beauties year-round. After the fall
American-grown crop is
consumed, the harvest from New
Zealand and Australia arrives in
spring.*

Baked Cinnamon Apples

Granola Crisp Topping with Fruit

⅓ cup old-fashioned rolled oats, uncooked
3 tablespoons chopped walnuts
¼ cup honey
1 egg white
¼ teaspoon vanilla
¼ teaspoon ground cinnamon
   Dash salt
2 cups nonfat plain or vanilla yogurt
2 cups mixed berries

Combine oats and walnuts in medium bowl. Mix together honey, egg white, vanilla, cinnamon and salt in small bowl until well blended. Add honey mixture to oats; stir until well blended. Line 11×17-inch baking sheet with foil; spray with nonstick cooking spray. Spread oat mixture in even layer on prepared baking sheet. Bake at 325°F 15 to 17 minutes or until golden brown, tossing mixture 3 to 4 times during baking. Remove from oven. Cool completely until crisp and crunchy. Serve over yogurt and berries.   *Makes 4 servings*

Favorite recipe from **National Honey Board**

Chef's Suggestion

Lining the pan with foil saves time on your clean-up. Just throw out the foil. There is no sticky mess!

Granola Crisp Topping with Fruit

Chocolate Banana Split Cake

1 sheet (18×12 inches) nonstick foil or heavy-duty foil, lightly
    sprayed with nonstick cooking spray
1 cup packed brown sugar
½ cup unsalted butter, softened
2 eggs
2 very ripe bananas, mashed
¼ teaspoon banana or coconut extract (optional)
1 cup all-purpose flour
5 tablespoon unsweetened cocoa powder
¾ teaspoon baking soda
¼ teaspoon salt
1 pint strawberries, halved
2 firm bananas, sliced
    Chopped nuts
    Whipped cream or whipped topping
    Chocolate Syrup

1. Preheat oven to 350°F. Center foil over 9×5×3-inch loaf pan. Gently ease foil into pan; leaving a 1-inch overhang on sides of pan and 5-inch overhand on ends.

2. Beat brown sugar and butter in large bowl with electric mixer at medium speed until light and fluffy. Add eggs; beat until smooth. Add 2 mashed bananas; beat until blended. Beat in extract, if desired.

3. Combine flour, cocoa, baking soda and salt in medium bowl. Gradually add dry ingredients to creamed mixture, beating until smooth.

4. Pour batter into prepared pan. Fold foil over batter to cover batter completely; crimp foil, leaving head space for cake as it rises.

5. Bake 1 hour and 15 minutes or until toothpick inserted into center comes out clean. Cool 10 minutes on wire rack. Open foil and lift cake from pan. Cool completely.

6. Slice cake into 8 (1-inch thick) slices. Serve with strawberries, sliced bananas, whipped topping, nuts and drizzle of chocolate syrup.

Makes 8 servings

Acknowledgments

The publisher would like to thank the companies and organizations listed below for the use of their recipes and photographs in this publication.

BC-USA, Inc.

Cherry Marketing Institute

ConAgra Foods®

Filippo Berio® Olive Oil

Hebrew National®

Hershey Foods Corporation

Hillshire Farm®

Hormel Foods, LLC

The Kingsford Products Company

Lawry's® Foods

Mrs. Dash®

National Chicken Council / US Poultry & Egg Association

National Honey Board

National Pork Board

Perdue Farms Incorporated

Reckitt Benckiser Inc.

The J.M. Smucker Company

StarKist® Seafood Company

Reprinted with permission of Sunkist Growers, Inc.

Uncle Ben's Inc.

Unilever Bestfoods North America

Veg•All®

Index

METRIC CONVERSION CHART

VOLUME MEASUREMENTS (dry)

¹/₈ teaspoon = 0.5 mL
¹/₄ teaspoon = 1 mL
¹/₂ teaspoon = 2 mL
³/₄ teaspoon = 4 mL
1 teaspoon = 5 mL
1 tablespoon = 15 mL
2 tablespoons = 30 mL
¹/₄ cup = 60 mL
¹/₃ cup = 75 mL
¹/₂ cup = 125 mL
²/₃ cup = 150 mL
³/₄ cup = 175 mL
1 cup = 250 mL
2 cups = 1 pint = 500 mL
3 cups = 750 mL
4 cups = 1 quart = 1 L

VOLUME MEASUREMENTS (fluid)

1 fluid ounce (2 tablespoons) = 30 mL
4 fluid ounces (¹/₂ cup) = 125 mL
8 fluid ounces (1 cup) = 250 mL
12 fluid ounces (1¹/₂ cups) = 375 mL
16 fluid ounces (2 cups) = 500 mL

WEIGHTS (mass)

¹/₂ ounce = 15 g
1 ounce = 30 g
3 ounces = 90 g
4 ounces = 120 g
8 ounces = 225 g
10 ounces = 285 g
12 ounces = 360 g
16 ounces = 1 pound = 450 g

DIMENSIONS

¹/₁₆ inch = 2 mm
¹/₈ inch = 3 mm
¹/₄ inch = 6 mm
¹/₂ inch = 1.5 cm
³/₄ inch = 2 cm
1 inch = 2.5 cm

OVEN TEMPERATURES

250°F = 120°C
275°F = 140°C
300°F = 150°C
325°F = 160°C
350°F = 180°C
375°F = 190°C
400°F = 200°C
425°F = 220°C
450°F = 230°C

BAKING PAN SIZES

Utensil	Size in Inches/Quarts	Metric Volume	Size in Centimeters
Baking or Cake Pan (square or rectangular)	8×8×2	2 L	20×20×5
	9×9×2	2.5 L	23×23×5
	12×8×2	3 L	30×20×5
	13×9×2	3.5 L	33×23×5
Loaf Pan	8×4×3	1.5 L	20×10×7
	9×5×3	2 L	23×13×7
Round Layer Cake Pan	8×1½	1.2 L	20×4
	9×1½	1.5 L	23×4
Pie Plate	8×1¼	750 mL	20×3
	9×1¼	1 L	23×3
Baking Dish or Casserole	1 quart	1 L	—
	1½ quart	1.5 L	—
	2 quart	2 L	—